W9-AOB-429

Endangered Species

Species

2nd EDITION

Endangered Species

2nd EDITION

VOLUME 3
Amphibians,
Fish, Plants,
and Reptiles

Sonia Benson,
Rob Nagel

Detroit • New York • San Diego • San Francisco • Cleveland • New Haven, Conn. • Waterville, Maine • London • Munich

THOMSON ™
GALE

Endangered Species, 2nd Edition

Sonia Benson and Rob Nagel

Project Editors
Julie L. Carnagie, Allison McNeill

Editorial
Diane Sawinski, Sarah Hermsen

Permissions
Margaret Chamberlain

Imaging and Multimedia
Robyn Young

Product Design
Michelle DiMercurio, Kate Scheible

Composition
Evi Seoud

Manufacturing
Rita Wimberley

LIBRARY OF CONGRESS CATALOGING-IN-PUBLICATION DATA

Benson, Sonia.
    Endangered species / Sonia Benson ; Julie L. Carnagie, project editor. — 2nd ed.
      p. cm.
    Rev. ed. of: Endangered species / Rob Nagel. ©1999.
    Summary: Entries on more than 200 extinct, endangered, vulnerable, and threatened animals and plants describe the individual species, its habitat and current distribution, and efforts to protect and preserve it.
Includes bibliographical references.
    ISBN 0-7876-7618-7 (set : hardcover) — ISBN 0-7876-7619-5 (vol. 1) —
    ISBN 0-7876-7620-9 (vol. 2) — ISBN 0-7876-7621-7 (vol. 3)
    1. Endangered species—Juvenile literature. [1. Endangered species—Encyclopedias.] I. Carnagie, Julie. II. Nagel, Rob. Endangered species. III. Title.
QL83.N35 2003
333.95'42—dc22
                                                 2003016691

Contents

VOLUME 2: Arachnids, Birds, Crustaceans, Insects, and Mollusks

VOLUME 3: Amphibians, Fish, Plants, and Reptiles

Fish

Plants

Reader's Guide

Endangered Species, 2nd Edition, presents information on endangered and threatened mammals, birds, reptiles, amphibians, fish, mollusks, insects, arachnids, crustaceans, and plants. Its 240 entries were chosen to give a glimpse of the broad range of species currently facing endangerment. While well-publicized examples such as the American bison, northern spotted owl, and gray wolf are examined, so, too, are less conspicuous—yet no less threatened—species such as the Australian ant, Cape vulture, freshwater sawfish, and Peebles Navajo cactus.

The entries are spread across three volumes and are divided into sections by classes. Within each class, species are arranged alphabetically by common name.

Each entry begins with the species's common and scientific names. A fact box containing classification information—phylum (or division), class, order, and family—for that species follows. The box also lists the current status of the species in the wild according to the International Union for Conservation of Nature and Natural Resources (IUCN) and the U.S. Fish and Wildlife Service (which administers the Endangered Species Act). Finally, the box lists the country or countries where the species currently ranges.

Locator maps outlining the range of a particular species are included in each entry to help users find unfamiliar countries or locations. In most entries, a color photo provides a more concrete visualization of the species. Sidebar boxes containing interesting and related information are also included in some entries.

Each entry is broken into three sections:

- The information under the subhead **Description and Biology** provides a general description of the species. This includes physical dimensions, eating and reproductive habits, and social behavior.

- The information under the subhead **Habitat and Current Distribution** describes where the species is found today, its preferred habitat, and, if available, recent estimates of its population size.

- The information under the subhead **History and Conservation Measures** relates, if possible, the history of the species and the factors currently threatening it. Conservation efforts to save the species, if any are underway, are also described.

Beginning each volume of *Endangered Species,* 2nd Edition, is an overview of the history and current state of endangerment and its causes and a discussion of the International Union for Conservation of Nature and Natural Resources (IUCN–The World Conservation Union) that includes a brief history of the organization, its current focus, and a brief explanation of the status categories in which the IUCN places imperiled species. The final section focuses on the Endangered Species Act, briefly examining its passage, purpose, implementation, status categories, and current state.

Each volume ends with a Where to Learn More section composed of books, periodicals, Internet addresses, and environmental organizations. The book listing is annotated. The environmental organizations list—a selected catalog of organizations focusing on endangered species—contains mailing addresses, telephone numbers, Internet addresses (if available), and a brief description of each organization.

Finally, the volumes conclude with a cumulative index providing access to all the species discussed throughout *Endangered Species,* 2nd Edition.

The scope of this work is neither definitive nor exhaustive. No work on this subject can be. The information presented is as current as possible, but the state of endangered species, sadly, changes almost daily.

A note about the 2nd Edition

Since the publication of *Endangered Species* in 1999, the endangered or threatened status of many of the species included in these volumes has changed. Through the efforts of conservationists and legislators, some of these species have recovered or were upgraded to a less threatened status. The Przewalski's horse, for example, was considered extinct in the wild in 1996 by the IUCN, but a program to reintroduce horses bred in captivity into their historical habitat was unexpectedly successful. By 2000, 84 Przewalski's horses had been reintroduced and 114 foals (baby horses) had been born in the wild. In the early 2000s, a population of around 142 Przewalski's horses roamed freely, and the animals appear to be doing better each year they spend in the wild. Other species have declined to the very brink of extinction. Some—like the scimitar-horned oryx—have dramatically fallen on the IUCN Red List. The status of the scimitar-horned oryx fell from endangered to critically endangered in 1996 to extinct in the wild in 1999. It is likely that, with a captive-bred population now being prepared for reintroduction to the wild, the scimitar-horned oryx will be upgraded on the Red List in the near future. There are also new stories in many of the existing entries. Chimpanzees and gorillas, for one sad example among many, began making the news in 2003 when a scientific study found that their populations had been reduced by nearly one-half since the 1980s and that an Ebola virus is currently ravaging the populations.

Endangered Species cannot cover all threatened species worldwide, but 40 new species have been included in the 2nd Edition to ensure that the situations of species worldwide—as it stands five years after the first publication—are represented. Conservationists today are facing the same concerns as five years ago, many with more urgency and some new twists. The issues range from a worldwide decline in the amphibian and reptile populations to declining fish species that seem unable to recover from overfishing; from the effects of inbreeding in populations that have become very tiny to the lack of appropriate habitats in which to release the new captive-bred populations. Many of the new entries chronicle the enormous efforts of scientists to save species on the brink of extinction. For instance, the Chatham Islands robin population had dwindled to five birds in 1981, with only one female, "Old Blue," remaining. Through a breeding-in-captivity program, that species now has 259 members, but all of them are direct descendants of Old Blue and her mate, Old Yellow. And sometimes these efforts may not be enough: There were only three Po'oulis (honeycreepers) left in 2003, and because their ranges did not overlap, they had no chance of mating in the wild. Scientists were preparing to take these last remaining members of the species into custody as the only hope for saving the species.

Acknowledgments

Special thanks are due for the invaluable comments and suggestions provided by the *Endangered Species* advisors:

Valerie Doud, Science Teacher, Peru Junior High School, Peru, Indiana

Melba Holland, Earth Science/Science Department Head, Slaton Junior High School, Slaton, Texas

Bonnie L. Raasch, Media Specialist, C. B. Vernon Middle School, Marion, Iowa

The editors of *Endangered Species* also graciously thank Tom Romig and Julie Carnagie for their commitment to this project and for their patience and understanding during its completion. It is a continuing privilege and pleasure to work with the U•X•L family.

Comments and Suggestions

We welcome your comments on *Endangered Species* and suggestions for species to be included in future editions of *Endangered Species*. Please write: Editors, *Endangered Species*, U•X•L, 27500 Drake Rd., Farmington Hills, Michigan 48331–3535; call toll free: 1–800–877–4253; fax: 248–699–8097; or send e-mail via www.gale.com.

Endangerment and Its Causes: An Overview

Living organisms have been disappearing from the face of Earth since the beginning of life on the planet. Most of the species that have ever lived on Earth are now extinct. Extinction and endangerment can occur naturally as a normal process in the course of evolution. It can be the result of a catastrophic event, such as the collision of an asteroid with Earth. Scientists believe an asteroid struck the planet off Mexico's Yucatán Peninsula some 65,000,000 years ago, bringing about the extinction of almost 50 percent of the plant species and 75 percent of the animal species then living on Earth, including the dinosaurs. Widespread climate changes, disease, and competition among species can also result in natural extinction. To date, scientists believe there have been five great natural extinction episodes in Earth's history.

Since humans became the dominant species on the planet, however, the rate at which other species have become extinct has increased dramatically. Especially since the seventeenth century, technological advances and an ever-expanding human population have changed the natural world as never before. At present, scientists believe extinctions caused by humans are taking place at 100 to 1,000 times nature's normal rate between great extinction episodes. Species are disappearing faster than they can be created through evolution. In fact, some biologists estimate that in the early 2000s three or more plant and animal species become extinct each day.

Because scientists have described and named only a small percentage of Earth's species, it is impossible to measure the total number of species endangered or going extinct. Just 1,400,000 species—out of an estimated 10,000,000 to 100,000,000—have been described to date.

Scientists do know that humans are endangering species and the natural world primarily in three ways: habitat destruction, commercial exploitation of animals and plants, and the transplantation of species from one part of the world to another.

Habitat destruction

The destruction of habitats all over the world is the primary reason species are becoming extinct or endangered. Houses, highways, dams, industrial buildings, and ever-spreading farms now dominate landscapes formerly occupied by forests, prairies, deserts, scrublands, and wetlands. Since the beginning of European settlement in America, over 65,000,000 acres of wetlands have been drained. One million acres alone vanished between 1985 and 1995.

Habitat destruction can be obvious or it can be subtle, occurring over a long period of time without being noticed. Pollution, such as sewage from cities and chemical runoff from farms, can change the quality and quantity of water in streams and rivers. To species living in a delicately balanced habitat, this disturbance can be as fatal as the clear-cutting of a rain forest.

As remaining habitats are carved into smaller and smaller pockets or islands, remaining species are forced to exist in these crowded areas, which causes further habitat destruction. These species become less adaptable to environmental change; they become more vulnerable to extinction. Scientists believe that when a habitat is cut by 90 percent, one-half of its plants, animals, insects, and microscopic life-forms will become extinct.

Commercial exploitation

Animals have been hunted by humans not only for their meat but for parts of their bodies that are used to create medicines, love potions, and trinkets. Overhunting has caused the extinction of many species and brought a great many others to the brink of extinction. Examples include species of whales, slaughtered for their oil and baleen. The rhinoceroses of Africa are critically endangered, having been killed mainly for their horns. Sharks' fins, cruelly cut off of the live animal, are used in Asia as an aphrodisiac, and 75 shark species are now endangered.

International treaties outlaw the capture and trade of many endangered or threatened species. These laws, however, are difficult to enforce. The smuggling of endangered species is a huge business. In the early 2000s, the illegal trade in wildlife products was estimated at $15 billion a year worldwide—second only to the value of the international illegal drug trade.

Introduced species

Native species are those that have inhabited a given biological landscape for a long period of time. They have adapted to the environment, climate, and other species in that locale. Introduced or exotic species are those that have been brought into that landscape by humans, either accidentally or intentionally.

In some cases, these introduced species may not cause any harm. They may, over time, adapt to their new surroundings and fellow species, becoming "native." Most often, however, introduced species seriously disrupt ecological balances. They compete with native species for food and shelter. Often, they prey on the native species, who lack natural defenses against the intruders. In the last 500 years, introduced insects, cats, pigs, rats, and others have caused the endangerment or outright extinction of hundreds of native species.

Endangered Species Fact Boxes and Classification: An Explanation

Each entry in *Endangered Species,* 2nd Edition, begins with the common name of a species, followed by its scientific name. Underneath is a shaded fact box. This box contains the classification information for that species: phylum (or division), class, order, and family. It also lists the current status of that species in the wild according to the International Union for Conservation of Nature and Natural Resources (IUCN; see page xxiii) and the Endangered Species List compiled under the Endangered Species Act (ESA; see page xxvii). (Note: For a listing of species whose status has changed since the publication of the first edition, see page xxxi.) Finally, the box lists the country or countries where the species is currently found and provides a locator map for the range of the species.

Classification

Biological classification, or taxonomy, is the system of arranging plants and animals in groups according to their similarities. This system, which scientists around the world currently use, was developed by eighteenth-century Swedish botanist (a person specializing in the study of plants) Carolus Linnaeus. Linnaeus created a multilevel system or pyramid-like structure of nomenclature (naming) in which living organisms were grouped according to the number of physical traits they had in common. The ranking of the system, going from general to specific, is: kingdom, phylum (or division for plants), class, order, and family. The more specific the level (closer to the top of the pyramid), the more traits shared by the organisms placed in that level.

Scientists currently recognize five kingdoms of organisms: Animalia (animals, fish, humans); Plantae (plants, trees, grasses); Fungi (mushrooms, lichens); Protista (bacteria, certain algae, other one-celled organisms having nuclei); and

Monera (bacteria, blue-green algae, other one-celled organisms without nuclei).

Every living organism is placed into one of these kingdoms. Organisms within kingdoms are then divided into phylums (or divisions for plants) based on distinct and defining characteristics. An example would be the phylum Chordata, which contains all the members of the kingdom Animalia that have a backbone. Organisms in a specific phylum or division are then further divided into classes based on more distinct and defining characteristics. The dividing continues on through orders and then into families, where most organisms probably have the same behavioral patterns.

To further define an organism, Linnaeus also developed a two-part naming system—called binomial nomenclature—in which each living organism was given a two-part Latin name to distinguish it from other members in its family. The first name—italicized and capitalized—is the genus of the organism. The second name—italicized but not capitalized—is its species. This species name is an adjective, usually descriptive or geographic. Together, the genus and species form an organism's scientific name.

How similar organisms are separated by their scientific names can be seen in the example of the white oak and the red oak. All oak trees belong to the genus *Quercus*. The scientific name of white oak is *Quercus alba* (*alba* is Latin for "white"), while that of the red oak is *Quercus rubra* (*rubra* is Latin for "red").

Since each species or organism has only one name under binomial nomenclature, scientists worldwide who do not speak the same languages are able to communicate with each other about species.

International Union for Conservation of Nature and Natural Resources (IUCN–The World Conservation Union)

The IUCN is one of the world's oldest international conservation organizations. It was established in Fountainbleau, France, on October 5, 1947. It is a worldwide alliance of governments, government agencies, and nongovernmental organizations. Working with scientists and experts, the IUCN tries to encourage and assist nations and societies around the world to conserve nature and to use natural resources wisely. At present, IUCN members represent 74 governments, 105 government agencies, and more than 700 nongovernmental organizations.

The IUCN has six volunteer commissions. The largest and most active of these is the Species Survival Commission (SSC). The mission of the SSC is to conserve biological diversity by developing programs that help save, restore, and manage species and their habitats. One of the many activities of the SSC is the production of the *IUCN Red List of Threatened Animals* and the *IUCN Red List of Threatened Plants*.

These publications, which have provided the foundation for *Endangered Species,* present scientifically based information on the status of threatened species around the world. Species are classified according to their existence in the wild and the current threats to that existence. The categories differ slightly between animals and plants.

IUCN Red List categories

The *IUCN Red List of Threatened Animals* places threatened animals into one of nine categories:

- **Extinct:** A species that no longer exists anywhere around the world.

- **Extinct in the wild:** A species that no longer exists in the wild, but exists in captivity or in an area well outside its natural range.

- **Critically endangered:** A species that is facing an extremely high risk of extinction in the wild in the immediate future.

- **Endangered:** A species that is facing a high risk of extinction in the wild in the near future.

- **Vulnerable:** A species that is facing a high risk of extinction in the wild in the medium-term future.

- **Lower risk: Conservation dependent:** A species that is currently the focus of a conservation program. If the program is halted, the species would suffer and would qualify for one of the threatened categories above within a period of five years.

- **Lower risk: Near threatened:** A species that does not qualify for Conservation Dependent status, but is close to qualifying for Vulnerable status.

- **Lower risk: Least concern:** A species that qualifies for neither Conservation Dependent status or Near Threatened status.

- **Data deficient:** A species on which there is little information to assess its risk of extinction. Because of the possibility that future research will place the species in a threatened category, more information is required.

The *IUCN Red List of Threatened Plants* places threatened plants into one of six categories:

- **Extinct:** A species that no longer exists anywhere around the world.

- **Extinct/Endangered:** A species that is considered possibly to be extinct in the wild.

- **Endangered:** A species that is in immediate danger of extinction if the factors threatening it continue.

- **Vulnerable:** A species that will likely become endangered if the factors threatening it continue.

- **Rare:** A species with a small world population that is currently neither endangered nor threatened, but is at risk.

- **Indeterminate:** A species that is threatened, but on which there is not enough information to place it in the appropriate category of Extinct, Endangered, Vulnerable, or Rare.

The IUCN issues its Red List assessments of animal and plant endangerment periodically. The Red List of 2000 revised the previous 1996 list. The trends shown in the 2000 report were not encouraging. In 2002, the IUCN listed 11,167 threatened species worldwide. Of these, 3,521 were vertebrates, 1,932 were invertebrates, and 5,714 were plants. The majority of these species were listed as vulnerable. From 1996 to 2000, the number of endangered species rose. Notably, the number of critically endangered mammals rose from 169 to 180, and the number of critically endangered birds rose from 168 to 182. Among mammals, there were dramatic population declines in amphibians, reptiles, and primates, among other groups. At the same time there was an upward shift in levels of endangerment.

Endangered Species Act

The Endangered Species Act (ESA) was passed by the U.S. Congress in 1973 and was reauthorized in 1988. The purpose of the ESA is to recover species around the world that are in danger of human-caused extinction. There are three basic elements to the ESA program: the creation of a list of endangered animals and plants (the Endangered Species List), the formulation of recovery plans for each species on the list, and the designation of critical habitat for each species listed. Through this program, the act seeks to provide a means of conserving those species and their ecosystems.

The U.S. Fish and Wildlife Service (USFWS), a part of the Department of Interior, is the federal agency responsible for listing (or reclassifying or delisting) endangered and threatened species on the Endangered Species List. The National Marine Fisheries Service is responsible for many species that live in the oceans. The decision to list a species is based solely on scientific factors. Once a species is placed on the list, the USFWS is required to develop a plan for its recovery and to designate "critical habitat" for the species. Critical habitat is an area that has been deemed essential to the physical and biological needs of the species, either in their original range or an area similar to it. The designated critical habitat must provide appropriate space for population growth and normal behavior so that a species may recover. The critical habitat designation does not prohibit human activity or create a refuge for the species. Once it has been established, however, any federal agencies planning to build on that land (a highway, for example) must seek the permission of the USFWS. Any other activities requiring federal permits must go through the USFWS as well. Private landowners are not affected, except that the designation alerts the public to the importance of the area in the species' survival. The ESA explicitly states that the economic interests of the human community must be given ample consideration in designating critical habitats and requires the balancing of species protection with economic development.

When a species is placed on the Endangered Species List, it is positioned in one of two categories:

- **Endangered:** A species that is in danger of extinction throughout all or a significant part of its range.
- **Threatened:** A species that is likely to become endangered in the foreseeable future.

The ESA outlaws the buying, selling, transporting, importing, or exporting of any listed species. Most important, the act bans the taking of any listed species within the United States and its territorial seas. "Taking" is defined as harassing, harming, pursuing, hunting, shooting, wounding, cutting, trapping, killing, removing, capturing, or collecting. The taking of listed species is prohibited on both private and public lands.

Violators of the ESA are subject to heavy fines. Individuals can face up to $100,000 in fines and up to one year's imprisonment. Organizations found in violation of the act may be fined up to $200,000.

In 2003 there were 1,253 species on the Endangered Species List. This total included 517 animals and 746 plants.

In the 30 years since its passage, the ESA has been continually targeted by its many opponents. Some of those opponents believe the ESA prohibits human progress, placing the rights of other species ahead of the rights of humans. There are many interest groups who lobby against the ESA: building and real estate development associations oppose ESA because it could present some federal impediments to the large financial gains to be made in constructing new communities or facilities; loggers, farmers, fishers, hunters, fur traders, and others whose means of making a living are affected are also heavily represented in anti-ESA activism. Politicians, even those who nominally support the ESA, do not often find it politically advantageous to provide the necessary support and funding to rescue little-known animals or to oppose large and powerful companies.

On May 28, 2003, the USFWS announced a moratorium (suspension of activity) on designating critical habitat for endangered species—a required step under the ESA. The Department of the Interior said that its critical habitat program had run out of money. Of all the 1,253 endangered species to date, only 426 had critical habitats, and since 2000, those had shrunk in size considerably. Large conservation groups had repeatedly taken the government to court for its failure to designate critical habitat for a listed endangered species. The courts continuously upheld the requirement under the ESA for the USFWS to designate critical habitat for a species once it had been listed on the Endangered Species List.

Spokespeople from the Department of the Interior contend that the critical habitation designation system is unreasonably expensive and that it is not effective in saving endangered species. They also argue that the cost of these lawsuits over critical habitat designation is depleting the budget for protecting species. Many environmental groups, however, argue that critical habitat designation, flawed though the program may be, has been effective in the recovery of many species. Since habitat loss is considered to be the largest factor in the recovery of endangered species, the limited power of the program to protect habitats often represents the only hope for many species. Many endangered species, even if their populations could be increased, are simply running out of places where they can survive in the wild.

In the early 2000s, the issue of endangered species has increasingly become one of the arenas in which U.S. political divisions are playing out very dramatically. In the meantime, some of the species included in *Endangered Species,* 2nd Edition, are losing the last few acres or streams or caves or hillsides they require to survive; others stand only a few individual animals away from extinction.

Changes in Status from First Edition

Key: OFF = Delisted because of recovery; LR–CD = Lower Risk, Conservation Dependent; LR–NT = Lower Risk, Near Threatened; TH = Threatened; R = Rare; VU = Vulnerable; EN = Endangered; CE = Critically Endangered; EXEN = Extinct/Endangered (plants); EW = Extinct in the Wild

Species That Moved to a Less Threatened Status, 1998–2003

Mammals
Horse, Przewalski's: EW to OFF (IUCN)
Wolf, gray: LR–CD to OFF (IUCN); EN to TH (ESA)

Birds
Albatross, short tailed: EN to VU (IUCN)
Egret, Chinese egret: EN to VU (IUCN)
Falcon, American peregrine: EN to OFF (ESA)
Ground–dove, purple–winged: CE to EN (IUCN)
Kakapo: EW to CE (IUCN)
Kestrel, Mauritius: EN to VU (IUCN)
Lovebird, black-cheeked: EN to VU (IUCN)
Pelican Dalmatian: VU to LR–CD (IUCN)
Vireo, black-capped: EN to VU (IUCN)
Woodpecker, ivory-billed: EW to CE (IUCN)

Plants
Aloe, spiral Aloe: EN to OFF (IUCN)
Cactus, agave living–rock: EN to VU (IUCN)
Cactus, Peebles Navajo: VU to OFF (IUCN)
Cinquefoil, Robbins': EN to OFF (IUCN); EN to OFF (ESA)
Palm, Argun: EXEN to CE (IUCN)

Reptiles
Caiman, black: EN to LR–CD (IUCN)

Species That Moved to a More Threatened Status, 1998–2004

Mammals
Addax: EN to CE (IUCN)
Camel, bactrian: EN to CE (IUCN)
Jaguar: LR–NT to NT (IUCN)
Mandrill: LR–NT to VU (IUCN)
Monkey, woolly spider: EN to CE (IUCN)
Orangutan: VU to EN (IUCN)
Oryx, scimitar-horned: CE to EW (IUCN)
Tapir, Central American: VU to EN (IUCN)

Arachnids
No-eyed big-eyed cave wolf spider: No status to EN (ESA)

Birds
Booby, Abbott's: VU to CE (IUCN)
Crane, Siberian: EN to CE (IUCN)
Murrelet, Marbled : LR to VU (IUCN)
Parrot, Imperial Parrot: VU to EN (IUCN)
Penguin, yellow-eyed : VU to EN (IUCN)

Fish
Coelacanth: EN to CE (IUCN)

Plants
Cypress, Saharan: EN to CE(IUCN)
Fir, Baishan: EN to CE (IUCN)
Palm, Carossier: EN to CE (IUCN)
Rosewood, Brazilian: R to VU(IUCN)
Torreya, Florida: EN to CE(IUCN)

Reptiles
Leatherback Sea Turtle: EN to CE (IUCN)

Words to Know

A

Adaptation: A genetically determined characteristic, or inherited trait, that makes an organism better able to cope with its environment.

Alpine: Relating to mountainous regions.

Arid: Land that receives less than 10 inches (250 millimeters) of rainfall annually and has a high rate of evaporation.

B

Biodiversity: The entire variety of life on Earth.

Brackish: A mixture of freshwater and saltwater; briny water.

Browse: A method of grazing in which an animal eats the leaf and twig growth of shrubs, woody vines, trees, and cacti.

C

Canopy: The uppermost spreading branchy layer of a forest.

Carapace: A shell or bony covering on the back of animals such as turtles, lobsters, crabs, and armadillos.

Carnivore: An animal that eats mainly meat.

Carrion: Dead and decaying flesh.

Cetacean: An aquatic mammal that belongs to the order Cetacea, which includes whales, dolphins, and porpoises.

Chaparral: An ecological community of shrubby plants adapted to long, dry summers and natural forest fire cycles, generally found in southern California.

CITES: Abbreviation for Convention on International Trade in Endangered Species of Wild Fauna and Flora; an international agreement by 143 nations to prohibit trade of endangered wildlife.

Clear-cutting: The process of cutting down all the trees in a forest area.

Clutch: The number of eggs produced or incubated at one time.

Competitor: A species that may compete for the same resources as another species.

Conservation: The management and protection of the natural world.

Critical habitat: A designated area considered necessary for the protection and preservation of a species that has been listed under the Endangered Species Act in the United States. The area, either within or near the species' historical range, must provide an environment for normal behavior and reproduction so that the species may recover. The critical habitat designation does not prohibit human activity or create a refuge for the species. Once it has been established, though, any federal agencies planning to build or conduct activities within that area must seek the permission of the USFWS. The designation also serves to alert the public to the importance of the area in the species' survival.

D

Deciduous: Shedding seasonally; a tree whose leaves fall off annually or a forest made up of trees that shed their leaves annually, for example.

Deforestation: The loss of forests as they are rapidly cut down to produce timber or to make land available for agriculture.

Desertification: The gradual transformation of productive land into that with desertlike conditions.

Diurnal: Active during the day.

Domesticated: Animals trained to live with or be of use to humans.

E

Ecosystem: An ecological community, including plants, animals, and microorganisms, considered together with their environment.

Endangered: Species in danger of extinction in the foreseeable future.

Endangered Species Act (ESA): The legislation, passed by the U.S. Congress in 1973, which protects listed species.

Endangered Species List: The list of species protected under the Endangered Species Act.

Endemic species: A species native to, and found only in, a certain region.

Estivate: To hibernate (or sleep) through the summer.

Estuary: The place where freshwater enters the sea (e.g., at a river mouth).

Extinction: A species or subspecies is extinct when no living members exist.

Extirpated species: A species that no longer survives in the regions that were once part of its range.

F

Fauna: The animal life of a particular region, geological period, or environment.

Feral: An animal that has escaped from domestication and has become wild.

Fledge: When birds grow the feathers needed for flight.

Flora: The plants of a particular region, geological period, or environment.

G

Gene: The basic biological unit of heredity that determines individual traits. Part of the DNA molecule, the gene is transmitted from parents to children during reproduction, and contains information for making particular proteins, which then make particular cells.

Gestation: Pregnancy.

H

Habitat: The environment in which specified organisms live.

Herbivore: An animal that eats mainly plants.

Historic range: The areas in which a species is believed to have lived in the past.

I

Inbreeding: The mating or breeding of closely related individuals, usually within small communities. Inbreeding occurs when both parents have at least one common ancestor.

Introduced species: Flora or fauna not native to an area, but introduced from a different ecosystem.

IUCN: Abbreviation for International Union for the Conservation of Nature and Natural Resources; publishes *IUCN Red List of Threatened Animals* and *IUCN Red List of Threatened Plants*.

L

Larval: The immature stage of certain insects and animals, usually of a species that develops by complete metamorphosis.

Lichen: A plantlike composite consisting of a fungus and an alga.

M

Marsupial: Mammals, such as the kangaroo and the opossum, whose young continue to develop after birth in a pouch on the outside of the mother's body.

Metamorphosis: A change in the form and habits of an animal during natural development.

Migrating: The act of changing location periodically, usually moving seasonally from one region to another.

Molting: The process of shedding an outer covering, such as skin or feathers, for replacement by a new growth.

N

Native species: The flora or fauna indigenous or native to an ecosystem, as opposed to introduced species.

Nocturnal: Most active at night.

O

Old-growth forest: A mature forest dominated by long-lived species (at least 200 years old), but also including younger trees; its complex physical structure includes multiple layers in the canopy, many large trees, and many large dead standing trees and dead logs.

P

Perennial: A plant that lives, grows, flowers, and produces seeds for three or more continuous years.

Poaching: Illegally taking protected animals or plants.

Pollution: The contamination of air, water, or soil by the discharge of harmful substances.

Population: A group of organisms of one species occupying a defined area and usually isolated from similar groups of the same species.

Predator: An animal that preys on others.

Prehensile: Adapted for grasping or holding, especially by wrapping around something.

Pupal: An intermediate, inactive stage between the larva and adult stages in the life cycle of many insects.

R

Rain forest: A dense evergreen forest with an annual rainfall of at least 100 inches (254 cm); may be tropical (e.g., Amazon) or temperate (e.g., Pacific Northwest).

Range: The area naturally occupied by a species.

Recovery: The process of stopping or reversing the decline of an endangered or threatened species to ensure the species' long-term survival in the wild.

Reintroduction: The act of placing members of a species in their original habitat.

Reserve: An area of land set aside for the use or protection of a species or group of species.

Rhizomatous plant: A plant having an underground horizontal stem that puts out shoots above ground and roots below.

S

Savanna: A flat, treeless tropical or subtropical grassland.

Scrub: A tract of land covered with stunted or scraggly trees and shrubs.

Slash-and-burn agriculture: The process whereby a forest is cut down and all trees and vegetation are burned to create cleared land.

Species: A group of individuals related by descent and able to breed among themselves but not with other organisms.

Steppe: Vast, semiarid grass-covered plains found in southeast Europe, Siberia, and central North America.

Subspecies: A population of a species distinguished from other such populations by certain characteristics.

Succulent: A plant that has thick, fleshy, water-storing leaves or stems.

Sustainable development: Methods of farming or building human communities that meet the needs of the current generation without depleting or damaging the natural resources in the area or compromising its ability to meet the needs of future generations.

T

Taproot: The main root of a plant growing straight downward from the stem.

Territoriality: The behavior displayed by an individual animal, a mating pair, or a group in vigorously defending its domain against intruders.

Troglobyte: A species that lives only in caves.

Tropical: Characteristic of a region or climate that is frost free with temperatures high enough to support—with adequate precipitation—plant growth year round.

Tundra: A relatively flat, treeless plain in alpine, arctic, and antarctic regions.

U

Underbrush: Small trees, shrubs, or similar plants growing on the forest floor underneath taller trees.

Urban sprawl: The spreading of houses, shopping centers, and other city facilities through previously undeveloped land.

U.S. Fish and Wildlife Service (USFWS): A federal agency that oversees implementation of the Endangered Species Act.

V

Vulnerable: A species is vulnerable when it satisfies some risk criteria, but not at a level that warrants its identification as Endangered.

W

Wetland: A permanently moist lowland area such as a marsh or a swamp.

Endangered Species

2nd EDITION

FROG, CALIFORNIA RED–LEGGED
Rana aurora draytonii

PHYLUM: Chordata
CLASS: Amphibia
ORDER: Anura
FAMILY: Ranidae
STATUS: Threatened, ESA
RANGE: Mexico, USA (California)

Frog, California red-legged

Rana aurora draytonii

Description and biology

The California red–legged frog was, until recent decades, abundant throughout much of the state of California. It is the largest native frog in the western United States, ranging from 2 to 5 inches (5 to 13 centimeters) in length. The frog's skin is rough and thick and mostly reddish–brown or gray in color. It has dark spots with light centers on its back. Its upper abdomen is yellow, and its lower abdomen and hind legs are red. The frog's toes are only partially webbed (joined by tissues or membranes). It has vocal sacs, with which it makes sharp, low grunts during the weeks when it breeds.

California red–legged frogs eat invertebrates (animals without a backbone), small mammals, and other amphibians. Tree frogs, mice, and insects are common food items. Adult frogs are nocturnal (active at night), while younger frogs are active both day and night. Among the animals that prey upon California red–legged frogs are wading birds, snakes, and raccoons. When the frogs sense an enemy is near, they swim far out into the water and hide themselves in its depths.

California red–legged frogs breed from late December to early April. Mating is through external fertilization. The male takes hold of the female, she lays her eggs, and then he fertilizes them. The female lays her eggs in a mass ranging from 2,000 to 5,000 eggs. The eggs, which are dark brown and about .07 to .1 inch (2.0 to 2.8 millimeters) wide, are attached to vegetation, such as cattails or bulrushes, at or near the surface of the water. In a week or two the eggs hatch, and dark brown tadpoles (immature or newly hatched frogs) emerge. At the tadpole stage, the young frog has external gills and a rounded body with a long tail bordered by fins. It will remain in this form for 3.5 to 7 months. The tail and gills disappear and legs develop by the end of this period and the tadpole becomes a young frog.

Habitat and current distribution

California red–legged frogs live in rivers, streams, ponds, lakes, and wetland areas near the water's edge. They are found in central and southern portions of California, west of the Sierra Nevada Mountains up to an altitude of 4,000 feet (1,220 meters). The species currently occurs in about 238 streams or drainages in 23 counties, with the largest populations in Monterey, San Luis Obispo, and Santa Barbara counties. The California red–legged frog has disappeared from about 70 percent of its original habitat.

History and conservation measures

Before the nineteenth century, the California red–legged frog could be found throughout most of California, from north of the San Francisco bay area south to Baja California,

Mexico, and inland to Shasta County and the Sierra Nevada Mountains. The frog was common and familiar to most Californians, even making its way into Mark Twain's 1865 short story, "The Celebrated Jumping Frog of Calaveras County."

A large gold rush in the 1850s brought thousands of miners into California's Central Valley. The miners tore up the mountain streams in their search for gold, destroying large portions of the California red–legged frogs' habitat. Later in the century, frogs' legs became a very popular food item in San Francisco and the Central Valley. An estimated 80,000 frogs were killed for food each year. By the early 1900s, they had become harder and harder to find. To keep up with the demand for frogs' legs, bullfrogs were brought into California at the end of the century. Bullfrogs quickly became predators of the California red–legged frog, seriously reducing the

In the early 2000s, studies linked the losses in the California red–legged frog population to pesticides that were being used on nearby farms and were blown into the frogs' habitat.

population once again. Bullfrogs remain in the California red–legged frog's habitat and continue to prey upon the species.

After these early events seriously depleted the California red–legged frog population, loss of habitat and contamination brought the species to the risk of extinction. In fact, some of the worst damage to the species has occurred since 1985. Habitat loss due to the damming of waterways, livestock grazing, urbanization, loss of wetland environments, and agricultural development have led to the loss of 70 to 75 percent of the frogs' historical habitat. The introduction to California wetlands and streams of nonnative fish and bullfrogs, as well as alien plants, has further diminished the population. In the early 2000s, studies linked the losses in population to pesticides that were being used on nearby farms and were blown into the California red–legged frogs' habitat, contaminating it for the frogs.

The California red–legged frog was listed as threatened by the U.S. Fish and Wildlife Service (USFWS) in 1996. In March 2000, the USFWS designated 4.1 million acres as critical habitat for the California red–legged frog. Critical habitat is an area considered necessary to the conservation of the species. Critical habitat designation does not create a wildlife refuge and does not ban human activities in the area. Rather, it ensures that all federal agencies check with the USFWS about any activities they authorize in the area. A lawsuit was brought to the courts by a homebuilders association, which claimed that the USFWS had not adequately considered the economic impact of creating millions of acres of critical habitat. The courts agreed with the homebuilders association and revoked most of the critical habitat designation. This settlement, reached in July 2002, left as critical habitat 124,000 acres around Jordan Creek, a tributary to the Merced River in Tuolumne and Mariposa counties near the Sierra Nevada Mountains, and 75,000 acres in the Angeles National Forest near Los Angeles. The USFWS intends to propose a new critical habitat plan in 2004.

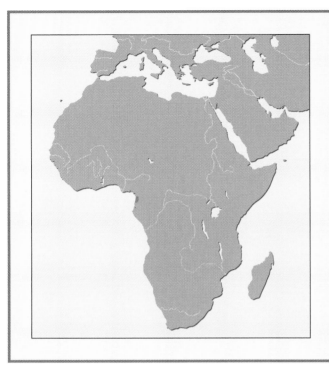

FROG, GOLIATH
Conraua goliath

PHYLUM: Chordata
CLASS: Amphibia
ORDER: Anura
FAMILY: Ranidae
STATUS: Vulnerable, IUCN
Threatened, ESA
RANGE: Cameroon,
Equatorial Guinea

Frog, Goliath
Conraua goliath

Description and biology

The Goliath frog is the largest frog in the world. It can weigh more than 7 pounds (3.2 kilograms) and measure almost 30 inches (76 centimeters) long with its legs extended. Its body alone can measure more than 12 inches (30.5 centimeters). The frog's upper body is greenish–brown in color, allowing it to blend well with the wet, moss–covered rocks on which it sits. Its underparts are pale orange or yellow. Its eyes can measure almost 1 inch (2.5 centimeters) in diameter. Males and females are very similar in appearance.

Adult Goliath frogs feed on insects, crustaceans, fish, and amphibians (such as newts, salamanders, and smaller frogs). Goliath tadpoles (immature or newly hatched frogs) eat only one particular plant found near waterfalls and rapids in their range. While smaller adults spend most of their time in water,

533

A comparison of a Goliath frog and a wristwatch. Weighing up to 7 pounds, the goliath frog is the largest frog on Earth.

larger adults frequently come out to bask in sunlight on rocks. The frogs are more active during the night, when they search for food along river edges.

The Goliath frogs' eggs measure about 0.3 inch (0.8 centimeter) in diameter and are surrounded by a jellylike substance. After mating, a female Goliath frog lays her eggs attached to grass or other vegetation along streams or the margin of rocky pools. Upon hatching, Goliath tadpoles are no larger than tadpoles of other frog species. The tadpole stage, in which the young frog has external gills and a rounded body with a long tail bordered by fins, lasts about 70 days. The tail and gills disappear and legs develop by the end of this period.

Habitat and current distribution

The Goliath frog has a very small range. It inhabits only a strip of dense rain forest in coastal sections of Cameroon and Equatorial Guinea in Africa. This area measures about 150 miles (241 kilometers) long by 55 miles (88.5 kilometers) wide. Within this forest strip, the frog is found only among a few swift–moving rivers flowing to the coast. These rivers are clean and well–oxygenated, and have an average temperature of 65°F (18°C).

The total number of Goliath frogs in existence in the wild is unknown.

History and conservation measures

The Goliath frog was first identified in 1906. Since that time, private collectors have paid large sums of money to own a specimen. In America, an adult Goliath frog has sold for as much as $3,000. There are no restrictions on the international trade of these animals. Luckily, they are not easy to find, despite their large size. Currently, Goliath frogs are found in only two zoos in the United States.

The primary threat to Goliath frogs is the destruction of their limited habitat. Many areas of the rain forest have been cleared to create farmland. To supply water to newly created farms and villages throughout the region, dams have been built across many rivers inhabited by the frogs.

Finally, as human populations have increased in the Goliath frogs' range, so has the demand for them as a food source.

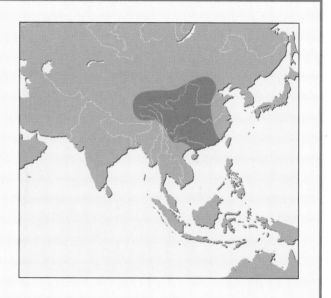

Salamander, Chinese giant

Andrias davidianus

Description and biology

The Chinese giant salamander is one of the largest salamanders on Earth (salamanders resemble lizards but have smooth, soft, moist skin). It has an average length of 3.3 feet (1 meter). Its head is broad and flat with a broad mouth. It has four short limbs and a tail measuring more than half of its total length. The Chinese giant salamander has smooth, rounded bumps (called tubercles) on its snout, at the edge of its eyes, and on other parts of its head. Thick skin folds with larger tubercles appear on the sides of its body. The upper part of the salamander's body is dark brown or pale brown in color with irregular black patches. It is lighter in color underneath.

The Chinese giant salamander is a carnivore (meat–eater), feeding on crabs, fish, frogs, shrimp, mollusks, and aquatic insects. It is especially fond of crabs.

During the breeding season, which peaks in August and September, a female Chinese giant salamander lays about 100

eggs in water. Each egg is about 0.3 inch (0.8 centimeter) in diameter; its cream color changes to white after it is laid. When the water temperature reaches 65° to 72°F (18° to 22°C), the eggs hatch within 45 days. The hatchlings, or newborn salamanders, are about 1.2 inches (3 centimeters) long.

Habitat and current distribution

The Chinese giant salamander ranges widely over Taiwan and north, central, south, and southwest China. There are no estimates of the total number of these salamanders in the wild.

The Chinese giant salamander inhabits mountain streams at elevations below 3,300 feet (1,006 meters). In these areas, plant cover is extensive and river water is shallow, cold, clear, and fast–moving. Deep pools and caves are abundant. The salamander seeks shelter in caves during the day and emerges to search for food at night.

Hunting is the main reason for the decline of the Chinese giant salamander population. The salamander's meat is said to be delicious and high in nutrients.

History and conservation measures

The primary threat to the Chinese giant salamander is hunting. The meat of this salamander is said to be smooth, white, delicious, and high in nutrients. In addition, humans in the salamander's range use other parts of its body to create medicines.

In 1989, the Chinese government listed the Chinese giant salamander as a second grade protected animal on its *List of Major Protective Wildlife of the State.* After this, many Chinese provincial governments also passed legislation to ban the killing of the salamander. Since the passage of these acts, dishes containing the salamander's meat are not served in large cities. In smaller cities and in the countryside, however, live Chinese giant salamanders or their meat are still sold.

SALAMANDER, SANTA CRUZ LONG–TOED
Ambystoma macrodactylum croceum

PHYLUM: Chordata
CLASS: Amphibia
ORDER: Caudata
FAMILY: Ambystomatidae
STATUS: Endangered, ESA
RANGE: USA (California)

Salamander, Santa Cruz long-toed

Ambystoma macrodactylum croceum

Description and biology

This species of salamander is so–named because of its long, slim toes. It has a thick body and measures just over 3 inches (7.6 centimeters) long. Its broad head ends in a blunt snout. The salamander is glossy dark brown to black in color with light spots.

The Santa Cruz long–toed salamander is primarily nocturnal (active at night). It feeds on insects (including their eggs and larvae) and vegetation. Garter snakes prey on young and adult salamanders; aquatic insects eat the salamander's eggs and larvae.

These salamanders migrate to their breeding ponds in November. Breeding peaks in January and February after winter rains have increased the size of the ponds. After mating,

female Santa Cruz long–toed salamanders will lay their eggs singly on stalks of spike rush or other vegetation below the pond's surface. Each female will lay about 200 eggs, which hatch in one week. The young salamanders metamorphose, or change from their larval state to their adult one, after 90 to 145 days.

Habitat and current distribution

The Santa Cruz long–toed salamander is found only in Monterey and Santa Cruz Counties in California. The total number of salamanders in existence is currently not known.

These long–toed salamanders require two distinct habitats. The first is a pond with a good amount of plant life for breeding, egg laying, hatching, and metamorphosis. The second is an area of dense vegetation relatively close to the pond that is used during the remainder of the year. This dry area also tends to contain mice, gophers, and moles that create burrows in the ground. The salamanders often spend much time in these burrows.

History and conservation measures

The Santa Cruz long–toed salamander was first discovered in 1954. Biologists (people who study living organisms) believe this salamander is related to a prehistoric species that was once widespread, but began to disappear after the beginning of the last major Ice Age (about 40,000 years ago).

This salamander is in danger of losing its habitat. Areas around the salamanders' habitat have been developed into farms and communities. Further development, including the building of a highway through the region, is a continuing threat. The runoff of pesticides from nearby farms also threatens to contaminate the water in the salamander's range.

In Santa Cruz County, the Elliott Slough National Wildlife Refuge and the adjacent State of California Ecological Reserve have been established to preserve the remaining Santa Cruz long–toed salamander habitat.

Salamander, Texas blind

Typhlomolge rathbuni (or Eurycea rathbuni)

Description and biology

The Texas blind salamander, which inhabits underground caves, has whitish, transparent skin. Its larger organs are visible through its sides and belly, giving its body a pinkish tinge. It has blood–red external gills and tiny gray dots covering its upper body. Two dark spots under the skin on the salamander's head may have been eyes at one time in this species' history. Its body is short and slender, and its large head has a wide, flattened snout. An average adult has a head and body length of about 5 inches (13 centimeters). Its tail, which tapers at the tip, is about the same length as the head and body. The salamander's long, slender legs resemble toothpicks.

The Texas blind salamander is a major predator in its underground habitat. It feeds on invertebrates such as shrimp

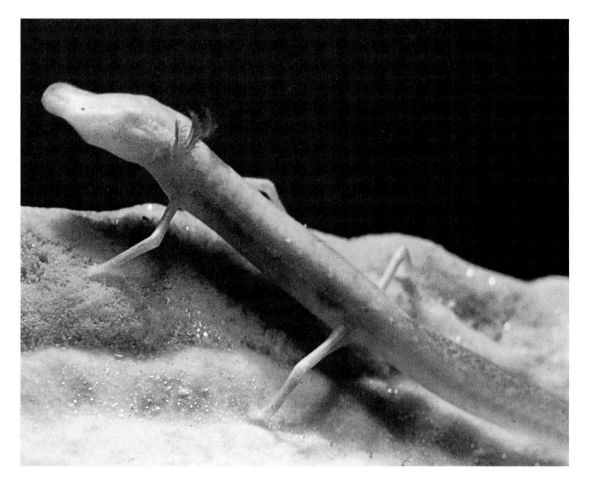

and snails. If the salamander is brought to the surface through a spring or well, however, it is an easy prey for fish.

Biologists (people who study living organisms) know very little about this salamanders' reproductive habits. They believe it is able to mate throughout the year.

Habitat and current distribution

The Texas blind salamander is found only in the San Marcos Pool of the Edwards Aquifer in Hays County, Texas (an aquifer is an underground layer of sand, gravel, or spongy rock that collects water). Biologists have no estimate of the salamanders' total population.

This salamander lives in the perpetual darkness of underground streams and caves. The water of its habitat is usually

A Texas blind salamander's transparent skin allows the visibility of its larger organs through its sides and belly.

very clean and has a constant temperature just under 70°F (21°C).

History and conservation measures

The Texas blind salamander was first identified in 1896. By the 1960s, it had begun to decline in number. The main reason was overcollection. Many scientists and hobbyists captured the salamander, fascinated by its physical appearance and ability to live in a cave environment. To protect the salamander from further collection, the only entrance to its habitat, Ezell's Cave, was declared a nature preserve.

The survival of this salamander depends on the quality of its water habitat. Farms and increasing urban development in its range now threaten the water. The water level in the aquifer continues to decrease as more and more water is used for human consumption and for crop irrigation. In addition, pollution from both urban areas and farms threatens to seep into the aquifer, destroying the Texas blind salamanders' fragile ecosystem.

TOAD, HOUSTON
Bufo houstonensis

PHYLUM: Chordata
CLASS: Amphibia
ORDER: Anura
FAMILY: Bufonidae
STATUS: Endangered, IUCN
Endangered, ESA
RANGE: USA (Texas)

Toad, Houston

Bufo houstonensis

Description and biology

The Houston toad is a medium–sized toad. Females average 2.1 to 3.1 inches (5.3 to 7.9 centimeters) long. Males are slightly smaller, averaging 1.8 to 2.7 inches (4.6 to 6.8 centimeters) long. The toad is usually light brown in color. Sometimes it has a reddish hue. It is covered with dark brown to black spots each containing one or more warts.

Adult Houston toads feed mainly on insects such as ants and beetles. Tadpoles (toads newly hatched or in their larval stage) eat algae and pine pollen. Some snakes and turtles may prey on the toad, and certain fish may prey on its eggs.

During mating season, males make a high–pitched trill to attract females. This calling can begin as early as late January, and breeding takes place when the air temperature reaches around 57°F (14°C). Females lay their eggs between mid–February and late June. Each female will produce 500 to

Conservationists are attempting to save the Houston toad by protecting its remaining habitat and reintroducing the toad into parts of its former range.

6,000 eggs. In order for tadpoles to develop, breeding pools must remain intact for 60 days.

Habitat and current distribution

Biologists (people who study living organisms) believe the Houston toad survives only in Harris, Bastrop, and Burleson counties in Texas. The largest concentration of these toads is in Bastrop County, particularly in Bastrop and Buescher State Parks. Biologists have estimated the total population there to be 1,500. The population in Burleson County is believed to be very small. Although no toads have been sighted in Harris County since 1976, biologists are hopeful that some still exist there.

The Houston toad occupies a variety of aquatic habitats, including lakes, ponds, roadside ditches, flooded fields and pastures, and temporary rain pools. Because it cannot dig burrows very well, the toad inhabits areas with sandy soil, such as pine forests. When not mating, the toad finds shelter in the sand, in burrows, under logs, or in leaf debris.

History and conservation measures

The Houston toad was discovered in the 1940s. Just one decade later, because of severe droughts that struck Texas, it was thought to be extinct. In 1965, it was rediscovered in Bastrop State Park.

This toad does not adapt well to dry and warm conditions, so these droughts severely reduced its population. Since then, the number of Houston toads has been further reduced as pine forests have been cleared to create farms and communities. The runoff of pesticides and herbicides used on farms and in residential areas also threatens to destroy what remains of the toad's habitat.

Conservation efforts for the Houston toad include protecting its remaining habitat and reintroducing it into areas in its former range.

TOAD, WYOMING
Bufo baxteri (hemiophrys)

PHYLUM: Chordata
CLASS: Amphibia
ORDER: Anura
FAMILY: Bufonidae
STATUS: Endangered, ESA
RANGE: USA (Wyoming)

Toad, Wyoming
Bufo baxteri (hemiophrys)

Description and biology

The Wyoming toad is rather small, having a head and body length just over 2 inches (5 centimeters). It is dark brown, gray, or greenish in color with dark blotches. Its belly is spotted and its upper body has numerous rounded warts. Males, which tend to be smaller than females, have a darker throat. This toad eats a variety of insects, including ants and beetles.

In May, males move to breeding sites and attract females with their calls. Breeding takes place up to mid–June. After mating, a female Wyoming toad will lay 2,000 to 5,000 black eggs in jellylike strings, often tangled among vegetation. These eggs hatch within one week. A tadpole (larval state of a toad) metamorphoses, or changes, into its adult state within 4 to 6 weeks.

Habitat and current distribution

Wyoming toads are found only at a lake and its surrounding wet meadows approximately 20 miles (32 kilometers) from Laramie, Wyoming. This site has an elevation ranging from 7,000 to 7,500 feet (2,134 to 2,286 meters). In the early 1990s, biologists (people who study living organisms) estimated that no more than 100 Wyoming toads existed at this site.

These toads breed along the borders of bays, ponds, and wet meadows, where water is shallow and vegetation plentiful.

History and conservation measures

The Wyoming toad was discovered in 1946. Despite its narrow range, it seemed to exist in great numbers. In the early

Recently, red leg, a bacterial disease, has been responsible for the decline of the Wyoming toad's population.

1970s, its population began to decrease drastically. After leveling off, its numbers began to drop again in 1989.

Biologists do not know the exact reasons that the Wyoming toad is disappearing. They believe it may be due to a number of possibilities. Pesticides used on nearby farms may have seeped into the toad's habitat, poisoning it. The toads may have succumbed to predators such as California gulls, white pelicans, and raccoons, all of which have increased in number in the toad's range. Changes in weather conditions, bringing longer dry spells, may have affected the toad's ability to breed. Biologists do know that a bacterial infection called red leg is responsible for the most recent decline in the number of adult toads.

Current conservation efforts include protecting and monitoring the remaining Wyoming toads and their habitat. A program to breed the toads in captivity and then release them into the wild has also been established.

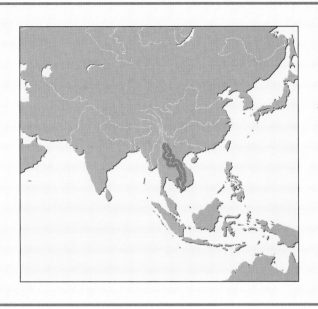

CATFISH, GIANT
Pangasianodon gigas

PHYLUM: Chordata
CLASS: Osteichthyes
ORDER: Siluriformes
FAMILY: Pangasiidae
STATUS: Endangered, IUCN
Endangered, ESA
RANGE: Cambodia, China, Laos,
Myanmar, Thailand, Vietnam

Catfish, giant
Pangasianodon gigas

Description and biology

The giant catfish is one of the largest catfish species in the world. It can grow to almost 10 feet (3 meters) long and weigh up to 660 pounds (300 kilograms). The fish has smooth skin and a short pair of barbels (slender feelers extending from the head near the mouth). Adult giant catfishes lack teeth. It is believed they feed on algae grazed from stones in the riverbed.

Biologists (people who study living organisms) have very little information about the location of spawning (egg–laying) grounds and the reproductive habits of this catfish. Adults are known to migrate upstream in northern Thailand in April and May. The giant catfish is the fastest-growing catfish species and one of the fastest-growing freshwater fishes. Catfish raised in captivity have reached a weight of 220 pounds (100 kilograms) in just 3 years. Biologists believe the fish grows even faster in the wild.

The giant catfish is one of the largest catfish species in the world. It can grow to almost 10 feet long and weigh up to 660 pounds.

Habitat and current distribution

The giant catfish is found in the Mekong River and its tributaries. Its range in the Mekong extends from the Vietnam–Cambodia border north through Cambodia, along the Thailand–Laos border and the Laos–Myanmar border, into Yunnan Province in China. It occupies the following tributaries of the Mekong: the Tonle River and the Tonle Sap (lake) in Cambodia; the Mun, Songkhram, and Kok rivers in Thailand; and the Yangpi River in China.

Adult giant catfish like to inhabit basins and deep depressions in large rivers in their range.

History and conservation measures

The giant catfish has been hunted for food for centuries. Although commercial fishing of the catfish had declined by the 1950s, it has recently increased.

Despite this increase, fishing is not a major threat to the giant catfish. What endangers this species more is the construction of dams along the Mekong to supply water to growing communities and farms in the region. Dams prevent the catfish from migrating upstream to spawning areas.

To keep the number of giant catfish from declining, the Fisheries Department in Thailand launched a captive–breeding program in 1967. In 1984, 80,000 of these captive–breed giant catfish were released into the Mekong. Two years later, that number increased to 300,000. Still, in 2001, catfish fishery in Thailand collapsed altogether due to the lack of fish. Numbers also dropped rapidly in Cambodia. The International Union for Conservation of Nature and Natural Resources (IUCN) began its process of upgrading the species status to critically endangered. Even so, in December 2003, the species' spawning grounds in the Mekong were due to be dynamited as part of a program of navigation channel improvements planned by the governments of China, Burma, Thailand, and Lao People's Democratic Republic. In the meantime, conservationists in Cambodia and Thailand were conducting migration studies and working with local fishers in order to try to save the giant catfish from extinction.

COD, ATLANTIC
Gadus morhua

PHYLUM: Chordata
CLASS: Osteichthyes
ORDER: Gadiformes
FAMILY: Gadidae
STATUS: Vulnerable, IUCN
RANGE: Oceanic: Atlantic Ocean, northeast and northwest

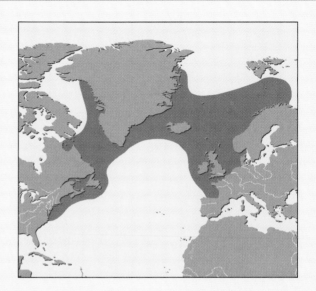

Cod, Atlantic

Gadus morhua

Description and biology

The Atlantic cod (sometimes called the North Sea cod) has been one of the world's major food fishes for centuries and is especially popular among Europeans and Americans. Tens of thousands of tons of this fish are caught every year, and thousands of people earn their living in the cod market. Atlantic cod are large fish: an average adult is over 4 feet (1.3 meters) long and weighs about 60 pounds (27 kilograms). Exceptionally large cod have been known to grow to about 6 feet (1.8 meters) and 210 pounds (95 kilograms). The Atlantic cod ranges from a dark greenish–gray to orange–brown in color. The upper body has spots across it, and there is a white line running from side to side. The fish has a stout body, a large head, and long barbel (a fleshy whisker) on its chin. Its fins—three dorsal (rear) fins and two anal fins—are all rounded in shape. Its belly is white.

The Atlantic cod is omnivorous (eats animals and plants). It generally feeds at dawn and at dusk. Young cod feed at the bottom of the ocean floor on small crustaceans, like shrimp or amphipods. Adults eat a great variety of mollusks, crabs, lobsters, and fish. Although cod do not form large schools for traveling, they do form small groups when they are hunting for food.

Cod travel long distances to their spawning grounds (the places where they produce their eggs) each year. Spawning generally takes place in the winter. The older a female cod becomes, the more eggs she will produce—a younger female may produce 3 million eggs, while an older female may produce 9 million eggs, in a season. Cod reach sexual maturity between the ages of 2 and 4 and they may live to be about 20 years old.

Habitat and current distribution

Cod live in a variety of habitats near shore and in the ocean depths. They are called "groundfish," because they stay near the bottom of the ocean much of the time. They generally prefer depths of about 200 to 360 feet (61 to 109 meters) in the summer and 295 to 440 feet (90 to 134 meters) in the winter. Their maximum depth is about 660 feet (200 meters). They prefer cool waters.

Atlantic cod occur on both sides of the North Atlantic Ocean. In the western North Atlantic, it occurs from Greenland in the north down to North Carolina in the south. In the eastern North Atlantic, it occurs from Iceland in the north down to the Norwegian Sea, to the Barents Sea and Spitsbergen (both north of Norway), and southward to the Baltic Sea and Bay of Biscay (on west coast of France). It is widespread all around the coasts of Britain and Ireland. In the waters off the United States, cod are managed as two commercial and recreational stocks: the Gulf of Maine and the Georges Bank (off the coast of Massachusetts) stocks.

DID YOU KNOW?

Since the late 1980s, many ocean fish populations have seriously declined. Some of the species threatened by overfishing besides Atlantic cod are: swordfish, black sea bass, red snappers, and some sharks. The populations are threatened by loss of habitat, pollution, and fishing practices that are not sustainable—that is, they allow fishers to take so many fish that the remaining population is unable to reproduce fast enough to make up for the ones taken.

Though the prospects for many of the endangered fish have seemed bleak, there is at least one case in which government–enforced fishing restrictions have successfully corrected the problem. The swordfish (*Xiphias gladius*) has experienced a dramatic recovery. In 1999, it was determined that the population had dropped to one–third of what it would have been without fishing. To continue existing fishing practices meant certain extinction for swordfish. A plan was enacted that limited fishing quotas to 10,160 tons (10,000 metric tons) per year. In addition, the United States closed 132,670 square miles (343,610 square kilometers) of swordfish habitat waters to longline fishing, in which the fishing line can be a couple of miles long and has baited hooks placed at intervals along its length. Remarkably, within just three years, the swordfish population has risen to about 94 percent of the number that scientists believe will assure the survival of the species if controls on commercial fishing are kept in place. Not all species have been so successful.

Scientists do not understand what is causing some of the deaths and illnesses among Atlantic cod. Many fish appear to be starving to death. Others appear to have developed a different body shape, perhaps to adapt to difficult conditions.

History and conservation measures

For centuries, abundant cod populations provided tons of food as well as reliable employment in cod fishery to thousands of fishermen in Europe, Greenland and Newfoundland, Canada, and the United States. Then, in the late 1980s, the cod fishery in most of the western Atlantic collapsed due to overfishing. The Atlantic cod population was in such decline that by 1992 moratoriums (enforced prohibitions) on cod fishing were in place throughout the northwestern part of its range. Even with the moratoriums, the stock in many places of the western sector has never recovered. The cod in the areas around Greenland and Newfoundland have experienced a 97 percent decline in population. Plans are in place to create protected areas for cod off the coast of New England. Canada's once–thriving cod industry has collapsed, and in April 2003, the Canadian government listed the Atlantic cod as an endangered species. The northeastern Atlantic cod population was later to experience the decline, but the fishing industry in Europe began to collapse in the early 2000s. In 2001 the stock was at such a low point that a large part of the North Sea was closed to cod fishing.

Overfishing is certainly responsible for the huge decline in the cod population, but the failure to recover stems from other very serious problems. Destruction of ocean habitat is one area of concern. A fishing technique known as "bottom trawling," in which fishers scour the ocean floor for fish, removes the cod's food sources and also eliminates places for young cod to hide along the ocean floor, so that they become easy prey for other fish. Pollution and climate changes are also likely causes of the population decline. Some species of seals, which are natural predators of the cod, are being blamed for the cod population's failure to recover.

Scientists do not understand what is causing some of the deaths and illnesses among cod. Many fish appear to be starving to death; they are found in very frail condition with emaciated bodies. Others appear to have developed a different body shape, perhaps to adapt to difficult conditions. In April 2003, hundreds of tons of Atlantic cod froze to death in the seas off eastern Newfoundland, and the incident remains unexplained. Scientists have also noted a mysterious lack of older fish in the cod population.

Since Canada imposed a moratorium on cod fishing in 1992, some populations of cod are beginning to recover, while others continue to decline. There are numerous recovery plans in the United States and in the other affected countries. On May 6, 2003, the European Commission met to launch a revised recovery plan for cod (Europe had already limited fishing in a temporary emergency plan). The cod catch in the seas off Europe is to be strictly controlled for a period of 10 years, with quotas set so that each year there will be 30 percent more adult cod than the year before.

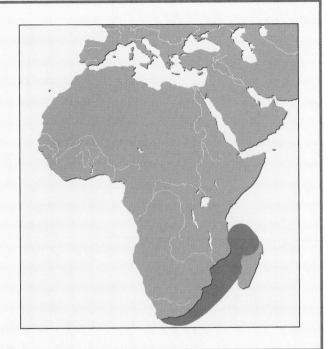

COELACANTH
Latimeria chalumnae

PHYLUM: Chordata
CLASS: Osteichthyes
ORDER: Coelacanthiformes
FAMILY: Latimeriidae
STATUS: Critically endangered, IUCN
RANGE: Comoros, Mozambique, South Africa

Coelacanth

Latimeria chalumnae

Description and biology

Biologists (people who study living organisms) call the coelacanth (pronounced SEE–la–kanth) a "living fossil." This fish is the only living member of an order that was abundant 80,000,000 to 370,000,000 years ago. A stocky fish, it is brown to steel–blue in color. It has large, rough scales and muscular lobes at the base of its fins. The coelacanth grows to a length of 5 feet (1.5 meters) and can weigh up to 150 pounds (68 kilograms). It feeds on lantern fish, cuttlefish, and other reef fish.

Like its relatives the lungfishes, the coelacanth can sense an electric field through an electroreceptive organ in its snout. When it encounters an electric field, it assumes an unusual "headstanding" position: it tilts so its head points downward and its tail points upward. Biologists believe this might be a technique the fish uses to detect prey hiding in the seabed.

A female coelacanth does not lay eggs, but gives birth to fully formed young after a gestation (pregnancy) period of over 12 months. Between 5 and 26 offspring are born at a time, each measuring about 15 inches (38 centimeters) long at birth. Young coelacanths probably live in caves and hunt at night. The fish reach sexual maturity at about 12 to 15 years of age and may live up to 80 years.

The coelacanth was once thought to be extinct, but scientists now know that the population of the fish numbers between 200 and 300.

Habitat and current distribution

Coelacanths have been found in the waters off the coasts of South Africa, Mozambique, and Comoros (group of islands between northeastern Mozambique and northwestern Madagascar). The greatest concentration of these fishes seems to be around Comoros, especially near the western coast of Great Comoro Island. Biologists have found it difficult to determine the exact number of coelacanths currently in existence. They estimate the total population to be between 200 and 300.

Coelacanths inhabit caves and steep, rocky drop–offs at depths between 400 and 1,000 feet (122 and 305 meters). Some of these fishes have been recorded at depths of almost 2,300 feet (700 meters). They congregate in caves during the day and emerge at night to hunt for food. A single coelacanth may cover a stretch of coastline over 5 miles (8 kilometers) in length in one night.

Habitat and current distribution

In 1938, an unusual fish was caught by fishermen off the eastern coast of South Africa. British amateur ichthyologist (scientist who studies fishes) James L. B. Smith identified it as a coelacanth. Scientists had previously thought this fish had been extinct for 80,000,000 years. In 1952, biologists found coelacanths living and breeding off Comoros. It was then discovered that native inhabitants of the islands had been catching and eating the fish for years.

Word of these discoveries soon spread. Museums, aquariums, and private collectors quickly sought the elusive fish, paying high prices. The number of coelacanths caught increased each year, reaching a high of 11 in 1986. In 1989, the Convention on International Trade in Endangered Species of Wild Fauna and Flora (CITES; an international treaty to protect wildlife) granted the fish Appendix I status. This banned the trade of the fish between nations that had signed the treaty.

In recent years, coelacanths have been caught and then sold illegally in eastern Asia. People in the region believe fluid from a certain part of the fish's body promotes longer life in humans.

The Coelacanth Conservation Council, established in 1987 in Moroni, Great Comoro Island, promotes public education programs coordinates research, and organizes protection efforts for the endangered coelacanth.

DARTER, FOUNTAIN
Etheostoma fonticola

PHYLUM: Chordata
CLASS: Osteichthyes
ORDER: Perciformes
FAMILY: Percidae
STATUS: Vulnerable, IUCN
Endangered, ESA
RANGE: USA (Texas)

Darter, fountain
Etheostoma fonticola

Description and biology

The fountain darter is a small fish that does not grow more than 1.5 inches (3.8 centimeters) long. It is reddish–brown in color with a series of dark, horizontal, stitchlike lines along its sides. Fine specks and dark blotches cover its back. Three dark spots appear at the base of its tail, and dark bars appear below, behind, and in front of its eyes. The black dorsal (back) fin has a broad, red band.

The fountain darter feeds during the day on aquatic insect larvae and small crustaceans, such as crabs or shrimps. It prefers only live, moving prey. The darter remains perfectly still, waiting for its prey to move within 1 inch (2.5 centimeters) of it, then it quickly darts or moves towards its prey (hence its common name, darter).

Female fountain darters can spawn, or lay eggs, throughout the year, but peak spawning takes place in late spring and again

561

in August. After a female lays her eggs on vegetation such as moss or algae, she abandons the nesting site and never returns.

Habitat and current distribution

The largest population of fountain darters is found in a 2–mile (3–kilometer) area of the San Marcos River in Hays County, Texas. A reintroduced population is found in the upper Comal River in Comal County, Texas. In the mid–1970s, biologists estimated that about 103,000 darters inhabited the San Marcos River. They believe, however, that the current population has increased slightly. The population in the Comal River is thought to be smaller than that of the San Marcos River.

Fountain darters prefer clear, clean water with abundant vegetation along the stream bed. Water temperature of their habitat is usually just above 70°F (21°C).

History and conservation measures

The fountain darter was first identified in the San Marcos and Comal Rivers in the late nineteenth century. In the mid–1950s, the fish disappeared from the Comal River when it was reduced to isolated pools. Droughts in the region had forced the Comal Springs, which feed the river, to stop flowing for a time. In 1975, biologists took a number of darters from the San Marcos River and reintroduced them to the Comal River.

Swimmers and other recreational users of the San Marcos River often disturb the algae mats used by the darters for nesting sites. However, the primary threat to the fish is the growing human population in the area and its increasing demand for water. This demand is depleting the underground aquifer (an underground layer of sand, gravel, or spongy rock that collects water) that feeds the fountain darter's river habitat.

State and local agencies that manage the use of the aquifer are developing water–use plans to help maintain spring flows to the rivers, and thus save the darter's habitat.

Pupfish, desert

Cyprinodon macularius

Description and biology

The desert pupfish is one of at least 35 species and subspecies of pupfish. Most are threatened with extinction. The desert pupfish is small, ranging in size from 0.8 inch (2 centimeters) to 3 inches (7.6 centimeters) long. It is mainly silver in color with six to nine dark bands on its sides. This pupfish has a short, scaled head with an upturned mouth.

The desert pupfish feeds primarily on brown and green algae. It becomes dormant during cold winter months, burrowing in mud at the bottom of its water habitat. When the weather and the water warms, the fish is active again and begins to mate. Breeding males turn iridescent blue in color and fight each other over the right to mate with receptive females. After having mated, females begin spawning (laying eggs) at the end of February. The males protect the eggs until they hatch three days later. Spawning continues throughout the summer.

The average life span of a desert pupfish is six to nine months, although some survive more than one year. Many die when intense summer heat dries up their streams and pools.

Habitat and current distribution

The desert pupfish inhabits the shallow waters of desert pools, marshes, streams, and springs below 5,000 feet (1,524 meters) in elevation. It can tolerate very warm and very salty waters. The fish inhabits only scattered areas in southern California and northwestern Mexico. Biologists (people who study living organisms) have no estimates of the desert pupfish's total population.

History and conservation measures

The desert pupfish was once common in the Sonoran and Mojave Deserts of southern California, southern Arizona, and

The draining and polluting of the desert pupfish's water habitat is the main reason for its population decline.

northwestern Mexico. Only three natural populations remain in California. In Mexico, natural populations survive in four locations. All natural populations of the fish were deemed extinct in Arizona in 1996. Efforts are underway to reintroduce the desert pupfish to various areas in Arizona.

The desert pupfish population has declined because human populations have increased in its range, turning desert areas into communities. As a result, the fish's water habitat has become polluted or has been drained. The pupfish has also been threatened by introduced predators and competitors such as mosquito fish, crayfish, bullfrogs, and snails.

The Dexter National Fish Hatchery and Technology Center in Dexter, New Mexico, maintains a population of desert pupfish.

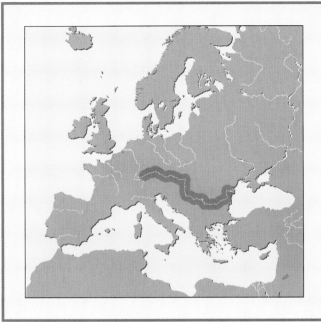

SALMON, DANUBE
Hucho hucho

PHYLUM: Chordata
CLASS: Osteichthyes
ORDER: Salmoniformes
FAMILY: Salmonidae
STATUS: Endangered, IUCN
RANGE: Austria, Bosnia and Herzegovina, Croatia, Czech Republic, Germany, Hungary, Poland, Romania, Serbia and Montenegro, Slovakia, Slovenia, Ukraine

Salmon, Danube
Hucho hucho

Description and biology

The Danube salmon, also known as the Huchen huchen, is the largest member of the salmon family. It can grow to almost 6 feet (1.8 meters) long and weigh 155 pounds (70 kilograms). It has a slender, cigar–shaped body. Its broad mouth contains a dense arrangement of teeth. This fish is highly predatory, feeding on fish, amphibians, reptiles, waterfowl (water birds), and small mammals.

Male Danube salmons become sexually mature at the age of four; females become sexually mature a year later. In the spring, females spawn (lay eggs) on the gravel bottoms of mountain rivers. After hatching, the young salmons develop very fast. After one year, they measure about 5 inches (12.7 centimeters) in length; by the end of their second year they have grown to almost 12 inches (30.5 centimeters) in length.

The Danube salmon is the largest member of the salmon family and is highly predatory, feeding on fish, amphibians, reptiles, water birds, and small mammals.

Habitat and current distribution

The Danube salmon was common in almost all rivers of the Danube watershed (the entire region drained by the Danube River). The salmon now breeds and spawns in only a few rivers in Austria, the Czech Republic, Slovakia, and Germany. It is found elsewhere in its range in only fragmented populations.

Danube salmons prefer cold, freshwater streams rich in oxygen and containing both rapid sections and deep pools lined with pebbles.

History and conservation measures

The greatest threat to the Danube salmon is the destruction of its habitat. Throughout its range, dams and canals have been built, preventing the fish from swimming to spawning grounds. Its habitat has been poisoned in many areas as sewage and industrial wastes have been pumped into rivers and streams. The runoff of pesticides from nearby farms has also poisoned many waterways.

Overfishing is a secondary threat to this salmon. Even though it cannot be taken without a permit and the fishing season has been shortened, the salmon's numbers continue to decline.

To help save the Danube salmon from extinction, conservationists urge that sewage dumping and pesticide use be controlled throughout the fish's range.

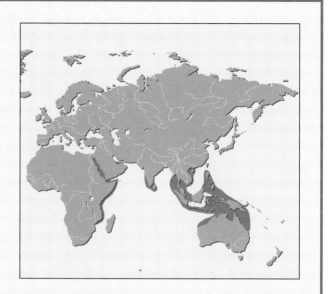

Sawfish, freshwater

Pristis Microdon

Description and biology

Sawfishes are large rays (shark–like fish that live at the bottom of the water) with long, flat, tooth–studded rostra (snouts). The unique snout, usually between one–quarter and one–fifth of the sawfish's total length, is used as a weapon to kill or stun prey (usually small fish) or to fend off the sawfish's enemies when they attack. It is also used to forage in the muddy bottoms of the water for crabs or clams. The freshwater sawfish (also called the largetooth sawfish) is a medium–sized sawfish, but it is the largest freshwater fish in Australia. An adult freshwater sawfish measures about 9.8 to 23 feet (3 to 7 meters) and can weigh over 1,325 pounds (600 kilograms). It looks like a slender shark except for its distinctive rostrum, which holds 14 to 22 modified scales that look like teeth. It is dark yellow to gray in color and has a white or cream–colored underside. This coloring, common among fish, provides safety: if looking down on the fish from above, the dark color of its back will blend with the darkness of the water; if looking up from be-

low, the lightness of its underside will blend into the light from the surface. Freshwater sawfishes have wide, triangular pectoral (front) fins and tall, pointed dorsal (rear) fins. Sawfishes have breathing openings behind their eyes called spiracles, which are used to inhale water. Their eyesight is good, but in the dark water at the bottom of rivers they must rely more on other senses. Fortunately, their rostra are so sensitive that sawfishes can actually feel the heartbeat of their prey in the water. Freshwater sawfishes have the ability to travel from the sea into freshwater as they choose.

Freshwater sawfish probably mate every other year. They produce baby fish, rather than laying eggs as some other fish do. The female produces anywhere from 1 to 12 young (usually about 8) at a time. Pup sawfishes are around 2.5 feet (77 centimeters) long at birth. They are born with a protective

Some of the biggest dangers to the freshwater sawfish are gill nets and trawling nets. With their saws, these fish become hopelessly entangled in any net.

covering over their saws, which are quite soft at the time of birth, probably to prevent injury to the mother. Their saws begin to harden quickly and the covering dissolves. They can begin to hunt small prey soon after birth. The freshwater sawfish reaches maturity at about 10 years of age and lives about 25 to 30 years.

Habitat and current distribution

The freshwater sawfish inhabits rivers, lakes, estuaries, and creeks. It moves between fresh and salt water easily, but probably prefers to sit on the bottom of shallow muddy rivers. It is not known to travel into the seas. Freshwater sawfish are found in fresh or brackish (part fresh water and part salt water) rivers in northern Australia, in Queensland, the Northern Territory, and Western Australia. They have been found up to 62 miles (100 kilometers) inland. The species has been known to range from southern Africa and eastern India through much of southeastern Asia to northern Australia, but appears to have disappeared from many regions where it once occurred. Australia may have some of the last healthy populations of freshwater sawfish.

History and conservation measures

All sawfish species are listed as endangered or critically endangered by the International Union for the Conservation of Nature and Natural Resources (IUCN). Some of the biggest dangers to the freshwater sawfish are gill nets and trawling nets. With their saws, these fish become hopelessly entangled in any net. Freshwater sawfish have also been hunted for their snouts, which are popular as souvenirs. Other parts of the fish's body have been used in traditional medicines. Overfishing has depleted the fish. Habitat loss is also responsible for decline in the population.

The freshwater sawfish was listed as critically endangered in Australia under the Environment Protection and Biodiversity Conservation Act of 1999 (EPBC Act). In Australia, research was underway in the early 2000s to determine which waterways were occupied by freshwater sawfish. One of the problems in trying to protect this rare fish is that little is known about it. Australian conservationists (people who work to protect and manage nature and natural resources) have launched studies in order to acquire much–needed data about the species and its habitat needs.

SCULPIN, PYGMY
Cottus pygmaeus (or Cottus paulus)

PHYLUM: Chordata
CLASS: Osteichthyes
ORDER: Scorpaeniformes
FAMILY: Cottidae
STATUS: Critically endangered, IUCN
Threatened, ESA
RANGE: USA (Alabama)

Sculpin, pygmy
Cottus pygmaeus (or Cottus paulus)

Description and biology

The pygmy sculpin is a small freshwater fish, averaging less than 2 inches (5 centimeters) long. It has a large head and spotted fins. Young pygmy sculpins have a black head and a grayish–black body. The adult sculpin has a lighter body and a white head with a few dark spots. These fish feed on a variety of insects, snails, and small crustaceans such as crabs.

Male and female pygmy sculpins both darken in color while breeding. Males become almost black and have a reddish–orange tinge along their dorsal (back) fin. Females may spawn (lay eggs) at any time during the year, but do so mostly in spring and summer. Sometimes two or three females form a communal nest by laying all their eggs on the underside of a single rock. Biologists (people who study living organisms) believe a male then guards this nest until the eggs hatch.

Habitat and current distribution

Pygmy sculpins are found only in Coldwater Spring in Calhoun County, Alabama. Biologists estimate that about 1,000 sculpins inhabit the spring run (small stream or brook) and another 8,000 inhabit the spring pool. Both the pool and the run have sand and gravel bottoms. The temperature of the water in each is a constant 61° to 64°F (16° to 18°C).

History and conservation measures

The pygmy sculpin was discovered in 1968. Because of its restricted range, it is especially vulnerable. Even though its population numbers seem high, the species could be wiped out if a natural or man–made disaster occurs at its site.

Conservationists (people protecting the natural world) believe the pygmy sculpin is indeed in danger. Evidence indicates that the aquifer (underground layer of sand, gravel, or spongy rock that collects water) that feeds the Coldwater Spring is becoming polluted.

SHAD, ALABAMA
Alosa alabamae

PHYLUM: Chordata
CLASS: Osteichthyes
ORDER: Clupeiformes
FAMILY: Clupeidae
STATUS: Endangered, IUCN
RANGE: USA (Alabama)

Shad, Alabama

Alosa alabamae

Description and biology

The Alabama shad spawns (lays its eggs) in rivers but spends some part of its life living in the ocean. It is a silvery-green fish that measures about 20 inches (51 centimeters) in adulthood. Females are larger than males. It has a distinctive pointed snout with a lower jaw jutting out from inside the mouth. It has 42 to 48 gill rakers, which are bony projections that point forward and inward from the gill raker arches to aid in the fish's feeding. (Gill raker arches are bony arches in the throat of fish to which the gill rakers are attached—bony fish usually have four gill arches.)

Alabama shad travel in schools. In the winter and spring, when the water temperatures are cool, the shad travel up rivers and streams to spawn. They prefer to spawn over sand, gravel, or rocky surfaces in a moderate current. The male and female will leave the area after the spawning is complete. The young remain in the stream for several months. The Alabama shad's life span is about six years.

Habitat and current distribution

The Alabama shad spawns in medium– and large–sized rivers. It can be found in the eastern part of the Gulf of Mexico, from the Mississippi delta east to the Choctawhatchee River in Florida and also in the Cumberland, Tennessee, Missouri, Arkansas, Ouachita, and Red rivers. The largest existing population occurs in the Apalachicola River in northwest Florida. The exact population of this species is unknown.

History and conservation measures

The decline in the population of Alabama shad began with overfishing in the nineteenth and early twentieth centuries. Other human–related threats began to disturb the shad's life cycle as the twentieth century progressed. Particularly damaging was poor water quality due to commercial and navigational dredging (digging up the bottom) of the sand bars that the shad use for spawning. However, the greatest cause of decline in the Alabama shad population in Alabama is the series of dams built in the Alabama and Tombigbee rivers. These dams block the fish from their travels to spawn in the Mobile Basin, the region where the two rivers drain in Alabama.

Recovery programs for the Alabama shad are not yet underway, and the fish was not listed under the Endangered Species Act as of the early 2000s, despite its endangered status on the International Union for the Conservation of Nature and Natural Resources (IUCN) Red List. However, the U.S. Fish and Wildlife Service was creating a status report on the Alabama shad, hoping to begin action to protect the species.

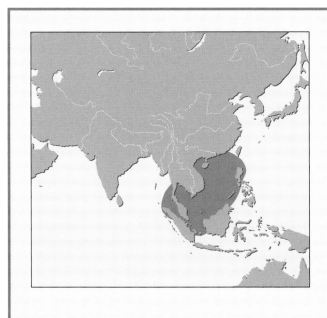

SHARK, BORNEO
Carcharhinus borneensis

PHYLUM: Chordata
CLASS: Elasmobranchii
ORDER: Carcharhiniformes
FAMILY: Carcharhinidae
STATUS: Endangered, IUCN
RANGE: China, Indonesia, Malaysia, Philippines

Shark, Borneo
Carcharhinus borneensis

Description and biology

The Borneo shark is a very rare species, little known to humans. It is not a large or dangerous shark. An adult measures about 27 inches (70 centimeters). In coloring, it is brown across the upper part of its body and white underneath. The markings on the shark are not very noticeable. The tips of its dorsal (near the back) fins are dusky and it has light edges on its anal fin. Wildlife biologists (people who study living organisms) do not have much information on the reproductive or other behavior of this species, but Borneo sharks are known to form strong male–female pairs. Fertilization is internal—the sharks do not lay eggs for external fertilization as do most fish. When the female gives birth, just a few young are born and they are developed at the time of birth.

Sharks have been around in largely the same form for at least 400 million years. Unlike most fish species, they have no bones. Instead, their skeletons are made up of cartilage, a strong but slightly elastic tissue. Sharks also lack a swim bladder, the air–filled balloon–like organ that keeps most fish upright. Without a swim bladder to keep them afloat, sharks will sink if they are not swimming. Most sharks must keep moving constantly because as they move forward with an open mouth, the water passing across their gills serves as their breathing. All sharks have jaws, and many have up to a thousand teeth arranged in rows. When the teeth are lost, new ones grow in to replace them.

Sharks play a crucial role as predators in ocean ecosystems. To save their energy, many sharks eat old, sick, or otherwise damaged fish—often whole schools of them—thus getting rid of the weaker populations and freeing up resources for the strong.

In recent times, the world's shark population has been in serious decline for a number of reasons; overfishing is the first. Shark became a popular food fish in the United States during the 1980s. By 1989, 16 million pounds of shark were caught by the United States in one year. A management plan for shark fishing was put into place that year. In 2002, however, conservation groups (organizations that work to preserve and manage the Earth's natural resources) charged the U.S. National Marine Fisheries Service with continuing to allow overfishing that was seriously depleting the shark population, especially off the coast of Florida.

Another cause of shark decline is a cruel practice called "finning." People catch a live shark, cut off its fin, and then throw the maimed fish back into the water. The shark, unable to swim without its fin, plummets helplessly to the bottom of the ocean and drowns. Shark fins are very popular in Asia. In some countries, shark fins in soup are thought to work as an aphrodisiac (something that arouses sexual desire). In fact, China and Hong Kong together in the year 1990 imported 5 billion pounds (2.2 billion kilograms) of shark fins. The United States has prohibited finning, but illegal finning of sharks is widespread.

In the early 2000s, the International Union for Conservation of Nature and Natural Resources (IUCN) listed 75 shark species as endangered. By one estimate, 100 million sharks were being killed each year for their fins and more for shark meat. Sharks do not reach sexual maturity until late in life (often at the age of 15) and they have long gestation (pregnancy) periods. Reproduction becomes rare because young sharks are caught by fishers and never have a chance to give birth. Thus, the shark populations have been unable to recover.

Habitat and current distribution

The Borneo shark is native to several inshore coastal areas of the Pacific Ocean, the Indonesian Sea, and the South China Sea. It has been found in tropical areas of Borneo (an island in the Malay Archipelago, formerly Malaysia) and

China, and some scientists believe it also occurs in Java, Indonesia, and the Philippines. Since these sharks are very difficult to locate and observe, wildlife biologists do not know the exact population of the species, but it has been estimated at less than 2,500 with a continuing decline in its numbers.

History and conservation measures

All that is known of the Borneo shark was learned from only five specimens, four of which were found in Borneo and one in China. These five specimens were all found before 1937. There were surveys of the shark collections in the markets of Malaysia, Thailand, Singapore, China, and Taiwan in the 1990s and there were no records of any Borneo sharks among them. Therefore, the IUCN has noted the possibility that the species may be critically endangered in the early 2000s.

STURGEON, BALTIC
Acipenser sturio

PHYLUM: Chordata

CLASS: Osteichthyes

ORDER: Acipenseriformes

FAMILY: Acipenseridae

STATUS: Critically endangered, IUCN

RANGE: Albania, Algeria, Atlantic Ocean, Belgium, Black Sea, Estonia, Finland, France, Georgia, Germany, Greece, Hungary, Ireland, Italy, Mediterranean Sea, Morocco, Netherlands, Norway, Poland, Portugal, Romania, Russia, Serbia and Montenegro, Spain, Sweden, Switzerland, Turkey, Ukraine, United Kingdom

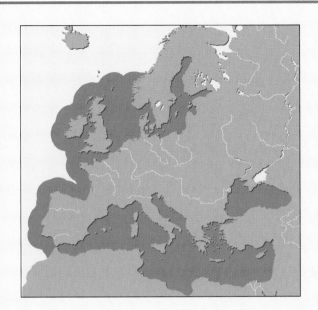

Sturgeon, Baltic
Acipenser sturio

Description and biology

The Baltic sturgeon is a large, slow–moving fish that may grow to a length of almost 10 feet (3 meters) and weigh up to 440 pounds (200 kilograms). It has a shovel–shaped snout with four fleshy barbels (slender feelers) extending outward from between the tip of its snout and its mouth. Five rows of bony plates line its body.

Young Baltic sturgeons feed mainly on insect larvae, mollusks, and small fish, while adults eat small fish, worms, snails, and crustaceans such as crayfish. These sturgeons probe the bottom mud and sand of their water habitat in search of food. Their sensitive barbels detect prey, which they then pick up with their protruding lips.

Adult sturgeons spend most of their lives at sea. In early spring of each year, they enter the mouths of connected rivers

to spawn (lay eggs). These rivers are swift–flowing, have gravel bottoms, and are 20 to 26 feet (6 to 8 meters) deep. After a female releases her eggs and a male fertilizes them with sperm, both return immediately to the sea. After hatching, the young sturgeons remain in the river or its estuary (lower area where it flows into the sea) for two to three years. Baltic sturgeons grow more rapidly than other sturgeons.

Habitat and current distribution

Baltic sturgeons are currently found only in scattered portions of their former range. The largest population now occupies the Black Sea. In the early 1980s, biologists (people who study living organisms) estimated that population numbered no more than 1,000. They now believe that number has dropped significantly.

In France, efforts are underway to develop a captive–breeding population to produce caviar (the eggs of the sturgeon eaten as a delicacy). Conservationists hope this captive–breeding population will also be used to repopulate rivers in which the Baltic sturgeon formerly spawned.

In order to spawn, the sturgeons need deep, fast–flowing rivers.

History and conservation measures

Baltic sturgeons were once widespread in the northeastern Atlantic Ocean and in the Mediterranean, Baltic, and Black Seas. They were occasionally caught around Ireland or off the coasts of northern African countries. By the 1970s, only single sturgeons were seen or caught in the Rhine, Po, Gironde, Danube, and Douro Rivers.

While overfishing has been a problem, this fish has declined in number mainly because its spawning grounds have been damaged. In some cases, breeding rivers have been altered, such as widened or deepened, to make them more navigable for ships. In others, locks and dams have been built on rivers, preventing the sturgeons from reaching spawning grounds. Many of the rivers in the Baltic sturgeon's range are now polluted.

The Baltic sturgeon is on the endangered species lists of France, Poland, Germany, and some countries of the former Soviet Union. In France, efforts are underway to develop a captive–breeding population to produce caviar (the eggs of the sturgeon eaten as a delicacy). Conservationists (people protecting the natural world) hope this captive–breeding population will also be used to repopulate rivers in which the Baltic sturgeon formerly spawned.

Sturgeon, pallid
Scaphirhynchus albus

Description and biology

The pallid sturgeon, also known as the white sturgeon, is so–named because of its light coloring. It is one of the largest fishes found in the areas drained by the Missouri and Mississippi Rivers. Some adults weigh as much as 85 pounds (39 kilograms). The fish's snout is long, flattened, and shovel–shaped. Its toothless mouth is located far under the snout. In front of the mouth is a row of sensory barbels, fleshy feelers the fish uses to detect food on river bottoms. It feeds on fish, snails, and crayfish and other aquatic invertebrates.

Males reach sexual maturity at 7 to 9 years of age, females at 15 to 20 years of age. Biologists (people who study living organisms) know little about the fish's reproductive habits. They do know that the sturgeon spawns (lays eggs) in June and July at the confluence, or junction, of the Mississippi and Missouri Rivers.

The pallid sturgeon, also known as the white sturgeon, is one of the largest fishes found in the areas drained by the Missouri and Mississippi rivers. Some adults weigh as much as 85 pounds.

Habitat and current distribution

The pallid sturgeon is found in the Missouri River and in the Mississippi River downstream from where the Missouri empties into it. The fish is also found in the lower portion of the Yellowstone River. Biologists do not know how many of these sturgeons currently exist.

Pallid sturgeons seem to prefer to inhabit the sandy or rocky bottoms of large, murky, free–flowing rivers. They have occasionally been found inhabiting sand flats or gravel bars in rivers, streams, lakes, and deep pools.

History and conservation measures

The pallid sturgeon was first identified as a distinct species in 1905. In the 1950s, its range included the middle and lower Mississippi River, the Missouri River, and the lower reaches of the Platte, Kansas, and Yellowstone Rivers. This range extended over a length of about 3,550 miles (5,712 kilometers). Now the sturgeon is considered one of the rarest fish in this range.

The sturgeon has declined in number because its habitat in both the Missouri and Mississippi Rivers has been drastically altered. Areas in both rivers have been dredged (deepened) to allow ships to navigate more easily. Dikes (walls built along rivers to hold back water and prevent flooding) and weirs (fences placed in rivers to catch fish) have been constructed throughout the fish's range. Other areas on these rivers have been enclosed in reservoirs or dams.

All of these modifications have blocked the ability of the sturgeon to swim throughout its range. They have also destroyed spawning areas and reduced the fish's food supply. In addition, portions of both rivers (especially the Mississippi) have high levels of pollution from industrial wastes and pesticide and fertilizer runoff from farms.

To prevent the extinction of this fish, the U.S. Fish and Wildlife Service is developing a captive–breeding program. Officials are hoping to use this program to reintroduce pallid sturgeons into former areas of their habitat.

DID YOU KNOW?

The sturgeon family, composed of 26 species, is a primitive family that has existed on Earth since the Paleozoic era (the division of geologic time occurring between 570 and 240 million years ago). Present–day sturgeons are remarkably similar in appearance to their prehistoric ancestors. Instead of scales, these fish have rows of armorlike bony plates, called scutes, which partially cover their body.

Sturgeons are found only in northern regions of Europe, Asia, and North America. Worldwide, almost every species of sturgeon is currently endangered. The demise of these fish began in the late nineteenth century, when humans began catching sturgeons solely to eat their eggs—a delicacy known as caviar. As a result, most species of this ancient fish family were brought to the edge of extinction in only 30 years.

SUCKER, SHORTNOSE
Chasmistes brevirostris

PHYLUM: Chordata
CLASS: Osteichthyes
ORDER: Cypriniformes
FAMILY: Catostomidae
STATUS: Endangered, IUCN
Endangered, ESA
RANGE: USA (California
and Oregon)

Sucker, shortnose
Chasmistes brevirostris

Description and biology

Suckers are large fish that feed by siphoning food with their mouths from the bottom of their freshwater habitat. The shortnose sucker differs from other suckers in that its mouth does not run straight across the end of its head but is tilted at an angle. It feeds on zooplankton (microscopic aquatic animals), algae, and aquatic insects. This sucker can grow to a length of 25 inches (63.5 centimeters) and live as long as 33 years.

Female shortnose suckers spawn (lay eggs) in the spring in rivers, streams, or springs connected to their lake habitat. A single female can lay up to 46,000 eggs during the spawning season.

Habitat and current distribution

Shortnose suckers prefer to inhabit freshwater lakes or reservoirs. They migrate up fast–moving connected waterways

to spawn. They are currently found primarily in Upper Klamath Lake and its tributaries in south–central Oregon. Smaller populations are located in the Clear Lake and Iron Gate Reservoirs in north–central California. In the mid–1980s, biologists (people who study living organisms) estimated that 2,650 shortnose suckers left Upper Klamath Lake to spawn. That number has decreased greatly in recent years.

History and conservation measures

The shortnose sucker was once common throughout the Upper Klamath River Basin (region drained by the river and the streams that flow into it). This basin once encompassed a drainage area of approximately 5,301,000 acres (2,120,400 hectares). The basin also contained over 350,000 acres (140,000 hectares) of wetlands and floodplains.

Biologists estimate that dams and other alterations to the shortnose suckers' habitat have reduced the fishes' ability to reproduce by as much as 95 percent. Unless spawning areas are reestablished for the shortnose sucker, its survival is considered unlikely.

Over the years, this area has been drastically altered. Dams were built on rivers to supply water to communities and farms. Irrigation canals were also constructed to divert water to farms. Wetlands, marshes, and floodplains were drained to create land for houses and farms. In the basin, only 75,000 acres (30,000 hectares) of wetlands remain. These changes have not only destroyed much of the shortnose suckers' habitat, but broken up any remaining habitat into sections.

The draining of wetlands has reduced the quality of water feeding the suckers' habitat. As water flows through wetlands into rivers and lakes, the wetlands act as a filter by capturing and neutralizing surface pollutants. Without them, the pollutants flow right through, eventually building to a point where they poison freshwater systems.

Dams have created reservoir habitats where the suckers can live, but they have also prevented the fishes from reaching their spawning grounds. Biologists estimate that dams and other alterations to the shortnose suckers' habitat have reduced the fishes' ability to reproduce by as much as 95 percent. Unless spawning areas are reestablished for the shortnose sucker, its survival is considered unlikely.

TOTOABA
Totoaba macdonaldi

PHYLUM: Chordata
CLASS: Osteichthyes
ORDER: Perciformes
FAMILY: Sciaenidae
STATUS: Critically endangered, IUCN
Endangered, ESA
RANGE: Mexico

Totoaba
Totoaba macdonaldi

Description and biology

The totoaba (pronounced tow–TOWA–ba) is a large fish with a compressed body. It can grow to almost 6 feet (1.8 meters) long and weigh about 300 pounds (136 kilograms). It is silvery–blue on the upper part of its body and dusky–silver below. It feeds on a variety of prey, including fish, crabs, shrimp, and other crustaceans.

The totoaba spends much of its life in the deeper waters of the Gulf of California (arm of the Pacific Ocean separating Baja California from the northwestern Mexican mainland). It spawns (lays eggs) in the shallow, brackish waters (mixture of freshwater and salt water) where the Colorado River empties into the gulf at its northern end. Spawning takes place from mid–February until June. After hatching, young totoabas remain near the mouth of the Colorado River. After about two years, they migrate south to join the parent population. These fish grow rapidly, reaching a weight of 50 pounds (23 kilograms) after just 6 years. A totoaba may live more than 35 years.

Habitat and current distribution

The totoaba is unique to the Gulf of California. It was formerly found throughout most of the gulf, but is now found only in the extreme northern end. To reach spawning grounds near the mouth of the Colorado River, totoabas migrate northward along the eastern coast of the gulf. After spawning, they return along the western coast to the colder, deeper waters of the gulf. Biologists (people who study living organisms) are unsure of the total number of totoabas in existence.

History and conservation measures

The totoaba, a good–tasting fish, was once hunted in great numbers for food and sport. In the early 1940s, the amount of totoaba taken from the gulf each year totaled just over 2,200 tons (1,995 metric tons). By 1975, the yearly take had fallen to just under 66 tons (60 metric tons).

The decline in the number of totoaba has been caused by overfishing and habitat destruction. Fishermen captured totoabas primarily during their annual migrations. This diminished the number of fish reaching spawning grounds. In the northern section of the gulf, shrimp boats accidentally trapped and killed up to 90 percent of young totoabas in their shrimp nets. Dams built on the Colorado River decreased the amount of freshwater reaching the Gulf of California. The water in many spawning areas dried up, while the water in others became increasingly salty.

In 1975, the Mexican government declared a total ban on all fishing of the totoaba. The following year, the fish was placed on Appendix I of the Convention on International Trade in Endangered Species of Wild Fauna and Flora (CITES; an international treaty to protect wildlife). This banned all trade of the fish between nations that had signed the treaty. In 1979, the totoaba was listed as endangered under the U.S. Endangered Species Act. Despite all these actions, the totoaba is still thought to be threatened by illegal fishing and accidental catches.

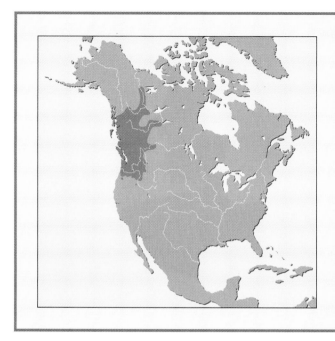

TROUT, BULL
Salvelinus confluentus

PHYLUM: Chordata
CLASS: Osteichthyes
ORDER: Salmoniformes
FAMILY: Salmonidae
STATUS: Vulnerable, IUCN
Threatened, ESA
RANGE: USA (Idaho, Montana,
Nevada, Oregon, Washington

Trout, bull
Salvelinus confluentus

Description and biology

Bull trout belong to a subgroup of the salmon family called "chars." Other char species are the lake trout, the Arctic char, and the Dolly Varden, which looks very similar to the bull trout and was once considered to be the same species. The adult bull trout weighs from 4 to 40 pounds (10 to 18 kilograms) and measures from 1 to 2 feet (30 to 70 centimeters) in length. Generally, bull trout are dark green to brown in color, with pale yellow and red spots and a white belly. There are many variations of physical characteristics within the species. Bull trout that live their lives in streams are generally quite small at around 4 pounds (2 kilograms). Bull trout that live in lakes grow to about 20 pounds (9 kilograms). The bull trouts' name was inspired by its large head and jaws.

Young bull trout eat insects. As they mature they begin to hunt other fish species, especially mountain whitefish, sculpin, and other trout. Bull trout have also been observed eating frogs,

Bull trout are adapted for life in very cold water. They are found in snowy mountainous areas in the deep pools of large cold rivers and lakes and in coastal and mountain streams.

mice, snakes, and ducklings. Most bull trout do not spawn (produce eggs) until they are five or six years old. Spawning takes place in the autumn. Bull trout need cold waters of about 48°F (9°C) in order to spawn. The female finds a small, spring–fed stream and digs out a nest in the gravel. There she will lay as many as 5,000 eggs. A male bull trout will release sperm to fertilize the eggs. The fertilized eggs are then covered with gravel. The male and female leave the eggs, which will incubate for five or six months, hatching in the spring. Some bull trout will remain in the stream for their whole life, while others will migrate to lakes and rivers and even to salt water areas to find food. They can live to be about 20 years old.

Habitat and current distribution

Bull trout, like other char, are adapted for life in very cold water. They are found in snowy mountainous areas in the deep pools of large cold rivers and lakes and in coastal and mountain streams. The bull trout ranges from northern California to southeast Alaska throughout many of the interior and some of the coastal river drainages of the Pacific Northwest. There are numerous subpopulations of the bull trout in Washington's Puget Sound area. In the United States, the bull trout currently occurs in Montana, Idaho, Oregon, Washington, and Alaska. In Canada, it occurs in British Columbia and Alberta.

History and conservation measures

At one time the bull trouts' range included large areas of the North American northwest, including the entire Columbia River Basin (region drained by the Columbia river and the streams that flow into it from British Columbia, Canada, south to Washington and Oregon), the Jarbidge River in northern Nevada, the Klamath River Basin in Oregon, and the McCloud River in California. In the beginning of the twentieth century, the bull trout experienced its first decline in population in some areas where sport fishing was popular when fishers began to stock new species of fish in streams and rivers. Since the bull trout ate other kinds of fish, including the new stock, fishers decided to try to eliminate the species from some streams to enhance their fishing.

Later, the bull trout has faced the threats experienced by many species: logging, mining, urbanization, pollution, damming, dredging, or altering the course of rivers, oil and gas exploration, and of course, overfishing. The bull trout, however, has very special needs because it is a cold–water species. Their eggs will not hatch in waters with temperatures slightly warmer than required. Changes in water temperature cause severe declines in the population. Pollution, siltation (water choked with too much sediment and fine rock particles) and a degraded stream habitat have also been responsible for a reduction in the bull trout population. In addition, bull trout have bred with some of the introduced species of trout in their habitat. These matches have produced sterile offspring.

There are many ongoing attempts throughout the bull trout's range to conserve stream habitats, not only for the bull trout but for other threatened species as well. Because there are several different types of bull trout—some migratory (traveling), some that remain in the stream in which they are born—threats to the species are varied, and each group needs separate actions to aid in its recovery. The U.S. Fish and Wildlife Service established 27 recovery units for the different large river basins where bull trout occur, each with its own recovery plan. The Canadian government has also instituted programs to protect the species, particularly by restricting fishing and educating fishers on ways to identify and protect the bull trout.

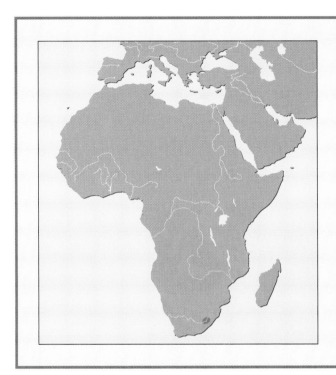

ALOE, SPIRAL
Aloe polyphylla

DIVISION: Magnoliophyta
CLASS: Liliopsida
ORDER: Liliales
FAMILY: Liliaceae
STATUS: Removed from IUCN Red List
RANGE: Lesotho

Aloe, spiral
Aloe polyphylla

Description and biology

An aloe (pronounced AL–o) is a succulent (a plant that has thick, fleshy, water–storing leaves or stems), native chiefly to dry warm areas of southern Africa. It is also classified as a perennial (plant that lives, grows, flowers, and produces seeds for three or more consecutive years).

The spiral aloe, also known as the kharetsa, has a rosette, or rounded cluster of 75 to 150 mostly erect leaves measuring up to 31 inches (79 centimeters) across. These leaves are arranged in five spiral rows, running clockwise or counter-clockwise. Each leaf is egg–shaped and very fleshy, measuring 8 to 12 inches (20 to 30.5 centimeters) long and 2.4 to 4 inches (6 to 10 centimeters) wide. The leaves have rather soft white spines or teeth on their margins or edges.

595

A flowering shoot extends 20 to 24 (51 to 61 centimeters) inches above the plant, branching from near the base. The flowers are clustered on the shoot tips. The color of the blooms can range from pale red to salmon pink. Very rarely, however, the blooms are yellow. Flowering occurs from August through December, with peak blooms visible in September and October.

Botanists (people specializing in the study of plants) believe insects and birds such as the Malachite sunbird help pollinate (fertilize by transferring pollen) the plant. The spiral aloe produces a large amount of seed, but it seems to reproduce mainly by sending out offshoots (shoots that branch out from the main stem of the plant to form new plantlets).

Habitat and current distribution

The spiral aloe is found in scattered areas in Lesotho, a country forming an enclave within east–central South Africa. The plant is concentrated in the Thaba Putsoa Range and the Maseru area of the Drakensberg Mountains. A survey in the early 1990s discovered an estimated 12,500 to 14,000 individual plants in about 50 areas.

The spiral aloe grows at elevations of 7,300 to 8,900 feet (2,225 to 2,713 meters) on steep slopes with loose rock. It is usually found on north–facing slopes. At altitudes above 8,600 feet (2,621 meters), it is found more often on easterly slopes. It grows in areas where its roots are kept moist in summer by a continual flow of water and where rainfall measures about 43 inches (109 centimeters) per year.

History and conservation measures

The number of spiral aloes in the wild has decreased mainly because the plants have been dug up for sale to gardeners and nurseries. With its striking arrangement of spiral leaves, this aloe is highly prized. Overgrazing by domestic animals on surrounding vegetation and the construction of roads have also destroyed much of the plant's habitat.

This aloe is the national flower of Lesotho and has been legally protected since 1938. In the early 2000s, these protections had advanced the population of this species to the extent that it was downlisted by the International Union for the Conservation of Nature and Natural Resources (IUCN). According to many conservationists (people protecting the natural world), however, greater protection against collectors is needed. At best, a national park should be established in which the spiral aloe would be protected from collectors and grazing animals.

BARBERRY, NEVIN'S
Berberis nevinii

DIVISION: Magnoliophyta
CLASS: Magnoliopsida
ORDER: Ranunculales
FAMILY: Berberidaceae
STATUS: Endangered, ESA
RANGE: USA (California)

Barberry, Nevin's

Berberis nevinii

Description and biology

Nevin's barberry is a large evergreen shrub with blue–green, spiny leaves, bright red edible berries, and bright yellow flowers that bloom March through April. It is a rhizomatous plant (pronounced RYE–zoe–mat–us; a plant having an underground horizontal stem that puts out shoots above ground and roots below) that measures from 3 to 12 feet (1 to 4 meters) in height. The leaves are pinnate, meaning they are arranged on opposite sides of the stem like feathers. The flowers are clustered, with six petals in two rows. The tiny, juicy berries are about 0.3 inches (6 to 8 millimeters) long.

Habitat and current distribution

Nevin's barberry is found in sandy or gravelly areas or in washes at altitudes ranging between 900 and 2,000 feet (300 and 650 meters) in chaparral habitats of the interior foothill region of southern California. The two largest populations of Nevin's barberry, together containing about 200 individual plants, are found near Vail Lake in southwestern Riverside County. Another large population occurs in San Francisquito Canyon in the Angeles National Forest in Los Angeles County. Beyond these three populations, there are some isolated populations in San Bernardino and Los Angeles Counties. Estimates of the total population place it at around 500 individual plants. Most of the Nevin's barberry habitat lies on private lands in the Vail Lake area, but some populations are located within lands belonging to the Bureau of Land Management, the Cleveland National Forest, and Angeles National Forest.

The range of Nevin's barberry has always been limited to specific areas of southern California, and scientists believe it has always consisted of fewer than 30 scattered populations.

History and conservation measures

The range of Nevin's barberry has always been limited to specific areas of southern California, and scientists believe it has always consisted of fewer than 30 scattered populations. At least seven former populations have become extinct. The biggest threat to these plants is urbanization, or the building of commercial and residential developments, within their small and specific range. The species requires certain kinds of soil, rock, and moisture, and a chaparral community of plants, to survive. It has been estimated that about 90 percent of the required habitat for this species has been eliminated by urban development, which includes building construction, road construction, flood control systems, and recreational activities, such as the use of off–road vehicles. Southwestern Riverside County developed at a very rapid pace and the Vail Lake area itself became a developing community in the 1990s. Land-owners whose property contains Nevin's barberry populations are likely to put in gardens and lawns, which will fragment the surviving populations and introduce nonnative plants to their habitat. The necessary fire management in areas developed for human residence and commerce is not like the natural fire cycles for which chaparral communities are adapted. There are no national recovery plans in place for the species, although research continues.

Cabbage, Lundy

Rhynchosinapsis wrightii

Description and biology

The Lundy cabbage is an herb with a slender taproot (main root of the plant growing straight downward from the stem). The plant is classified as a perennial (plant that lives, grows, flowers, and produces seeds for three or more consecutive years). Initially, the Lundy cabbage bears a rosette or rounded cluster of stalked, hairy leaves that measure 6 to 12 inches (15 to 30.5 centimeters) in length. As the plant matures, flowering stems rise stout and erect to a height of 3.3 feet (1 meter). These stems are woody, covered with downward spreading hairs, and have few leaves.

Flowers are clustered at the tops of the stems in groupings of about 20 blossoms. Each blossom has four long, yellow petals. The plant's seed pod measures 2.4 to 3.1 inches (6.1 to 7.9 centimeters) long and is very narrow. When it becomes dry, it splits open and releases round, purplish–black seeds.

Habitat and current distribution

The Lundy cabbage is found only on Lundy Island, located off the southwest coast of England. The island is about 1.5 square miles (3.9 square kilometers) in size. The plant is restricted to about 0.3 mile (0.5 kilometer) of cliff habitat in the southeast corner and to a few isolated areas along the east coast of Lundy Island. Botanists (people specializing in the study of plants) do not know how many individual plants are currently in existence.

The cabbage grows on east– and south–facing slopes and sea cliffs. It does not grow well in soils containing lime. It favors sheltered spots such as gullies, where it is damp in the winter and hot and sunny in the summer.

History and conservation measures

The Lundy cabbage is threatened by the presence of goats and deer on the island. Although sheep do not appear to touch the plant, they graze widely on the slope where it grows, trampling its habitat. The plant may also be threatened by the spreading growth of bracken (a large fern) and an introduced rhododendron species.

Lundy Island is owned by the National Trust of the United Kingdom, an association that preserves places of natural beauty or buildings of architectural or historical interest in the British Isles. The island is managed by the Landmark Trust. All vegetation and flora on the island are protected, and the cabbage population is carefully monitored. The English Nature Recovery Programme has recommended that bracken be cleared from parts of the island as a conservation measure to save the Lundy cabbage.

CACTUS, AGAVE LIVING–ROCK
Ariocarpus agavoides

DIVISION: Magnoliophyta
CLASS: Magnoliopsida
ORDER: Caryophyllales
FAMILY: Cactaceae
STATUS: Vulnerable, IUCN
RANGE: Mexico

Cactus, agave living-rock
Ariocarpus agavoides

Description and biology

Like all cactus plants, the agave living–rock cactus is a succulent (plant that has thick, fleshy, water–storing leaves or stems). It measures only 2 to 3 inches (5 to 7.6 centimeters) across. A stout stem grows up from the center of the plant. At the top of the stem is a rosette, or spreading cluster of fleshy, rough, gray–green, leaflike appendages. These measure 1.6 inches (4.1 centimeters) long.

Flowers arise from these appendages, blooming in November and December. The flowers, which open at night, are rose–pink to magenta (bright purplish–red) in color. They are funnel–shaped and measure 1.6 to 2 inches (4.1 to 5.1 centimeters) long. The fruits of this cactus are brownish–red club–shaped berries that measure almost 1 inch (2.5 centimeters) long.

Habitat and current distribution

This species of cactus inhabits the dry foothills of the Sierra Madre Oriental (a range of mountains running along the Gulf of Mexico) in the Mexican state of Tamaulipas. It is found mainly at an elevation of 3,900 feet (1,189 meters). A botanical survey in 1992 counted more than 12,000 individual plants. However, in 2001, the population of the species was estimated to be more than 100,000 individual plants, and in some areas they were reproducing at a healthy rate.

History and conservation measures

The agave living–rock cactus population has been reduced in number and continues to be threatened by collectors. It is highly prized by cactus enthusiasts because of its unusual shape. Urban expansion, rubbish dumping, and soil

The agave living–rock cactus population has been reduced in number and continues to be threatened by collectors. It is highly prized by cactus enthusiasts because of its unusual shape.

erosion have also contributed to the decline of this plant species.

This cactus is protected by international treaties, but illegal collection and trade continue. To ensure the survival of the agave living–rock cactus, legal protection of the species must be enforced.

CACTUS, PEEBLES NAVAJO
Pediocatus peeblesianus

DIVISION: Magnoliophyta
CLASS: Magnoliopsida
ORDER: Caryophyllales
FAMILY: Cactaceae
STATUS: Endangered, ESA
RANGE: USA (Arizona)

Cactus, Peebles Navajo
Pediocatus peeblesianus

Description and biology

The Peebles Navajo cactus is a small, globe–shaped cactus with no central spine. Like other cacti, it is a succulent (plant that has thick, fleshy, water–storing leaves or stems). It grows to a height of 2.4 inches (6.1 centimeters) and to a width of 2 inches (5.1 centimeters).

This cactus species blooms in the spring. Its yellow to yellow–green flowers measure up to 1 inch (2.5 centimeters) in diameter. The plant also bears berrylike fruit that turn from green to tan or brown when they ripen.

Habitat and current distribution

The Peebles Navajo cactus is found on low hills in Navajo County, Arizona. There are five known populations totaling around 1,000 individual plants. Two populations exist near Joseph City and the other three near Holbrook. The cacti

While most species of plants are pollinated by birds and insects, members of the Cactaceae family are pollinated predominantly by bats. One of the reasons is that bats are more prevalent than pollinating birds and insects in areas inhabited by cacti. Another reason is that most cacti open their flowers at dusk and hold them open during the night, a time when bats are most active. The pollen produced by cactus flowers is also higher in protein than those of plants pollinated by birds or insects. In this way, the cactus supplies the nutritional needs of the bats, insuring that they will return to help pollinate the plant in the future.

usually inhabit dry gravel soils at elevations around 5,600 feet (1,707 meters).

History and conservation measures

Excessive collecting and habitat destruction are the main reasons for the decline of this cactus species. Because it is so rare and is difficult to grow outside of its natural habitat, the Peebles Navajo cactus is sought after by private collectors and commercial plant suppliers. Areas where it grows are easy to reach, and overcollection could quickly wipe out this cactus.

Road construction, grazing animals, mining activities, and four–wheel–drive recreational vehicles have all destroyed part of the plant's habitat. Since the cactus can grow only in a specific type of soil, its habitat range is limited. Any destruction of that habitat will seriously affect the survival of the cactus.

Conservation efforts have been directed at protecting the Peebles Navajo cactus from collectors and preserving its fragile natural habitat.

CEDAR, BERMUDA
Juniperus bermudiana

DIVISION: Tracheophyta
CLASS: Coniferopsida
ORDER: Coniferales
FAMILY: Cupressaceae
STATUS: Critically endangered, IUCN
RANGE: Bermuda

Cedar, Bermuda
Juniperus bermudiana

Description and biology

When Europeans discovered the island of Bermuda in 1609, the landscape was dominated by Bermuda cedar trees (also known as Bermuda juniper). The species grew abundantly throughout the islands, with an estimated 500 trees to an acre in the many areas where it flourished. The large trees were useful as windbreaks, and protected early settlers from the sun and sea as well. They quickly became an essential part of the colonists' existence.

In good conditions, Bermuda cedars grow to about 50 feet (15 meters) tall, with a trunk measuring about 24 inches (0.6 meter) in diameter. However, where the trees are exposed to high winds or grow in scarce soil, they are smaller. They have a thin red bark that grows in narrow strips and weathers to a gray color. The foliage is dark and thick, with small, leafy branchlets. The leaves are like scales, overlapping each other. The trees produce dark blue seed cone, and dark purple berries.

Bermuda cedars have a strong, sweet scent. The wood repels moths and fleas and prevents mildew and rot.

Habitat and current distribution

Bermuda cedar is endemic (native to and only occurring in) Bermuda Island. It thrives in temperate lowlands and grows well on hillsides with limestone–based soils. A few stands of Bermuda cedar currently remain on the island of Bermuda, for the most part within its 12 nature reserves, and particularly within the 25–acre Paget Marsh Nature Reserve. Stands have also been planted on Nonsuch Island off the eastern coast of Bermuda.

History and conservation measures

In the early 1600s, colonists in Bermuda used the native cedar for building houses and ships; making furniture, medicine, and beer and wine; and as fuel. Soon after the first settlers arrived on the island, the forests showed signs of over-exploitation, and early measures were taken to protect these trees. In 1627, export of cedar for shipbuilding was restricted. By 1878, 16 more acts to protect the species had been passed.

As settlers from all over the globe arrived on Bermuda, foreign species were introduced to the islands. Starting in 1943, the accidental introduction of two scale insects (the oyster shell scale and the juniper scale, both in the form of fungus), devastated the Bermuda cedars. Within a period of ten years, 90 percent of the trees had been killed. An estimated three and a half million trees were dead due to the infestation of these insects. A few stands in remote areas survived.

The government of Bermuda has always been a leader in conservation efforts. In 1949, the Bermuda Board of Agriculture established its General Reafforestation Scheme, removing many of the dead cedar trees and replanting the cleared areas. The measures taken by the government have helped in some recovery of the species in the wild, and the Bermuda cedar population is now at about 10 percent of its population before the insect infestation. But the human population of the island has grown and the tourist trade has caused extensive development. There are only small, isolated areas of natural habitat for the once dominant tree, and there are many newly introduced species with which the Bermuda cedar must compete.

CINQUEFOIL, ROBBINS'
Potentilla robbinsiana

DIVISION: Magnoliophyta
CLASS: Magnoliopsida
ORDER: Rosales
FAMILY: Rosaceae
STATUS: Delisted, recovering, ESA
RANGE: USA (New Hampshire and Vermont)

Cinquefoil, Robbins'
Potentilla robbinsiana

Description and biology

Cinquefoils (pronounced SINK–foils) are members of the rose family. The Robbins' cinquefoil is an almost stemless herb that has a deep taproot (main root of the plant growing straight downward from the stem). It is classified as a perennial (plant that lives, grows, flowers, and produces seeds for three or more consecutive years). This cinquefoil has a dense rosette, or rounded cluster of crowded leaves, measuring about 0.8 to 1.6 inches (2 to 4 centimeters) across. The leaves, each composed of three leaflets, are deeply toothed along their margins or edges. They are covered with dense, long hairs.

The flowering stems are slender and only 0.4 to 1.4 inches (1 to 3.5 centimeters) long. Each stem bears a single small yellow flower, primarily in June. An average Robbins' cinquefoil produces five or six flowers.

Because the Robbins' cinquefoil has such a limited range, any human disturbance of its habitat has had a devastating effect. As a result of collecting by plant enthusiasts and trampling by hikers, several original cinquefoil populations died out.

Seeds are scattered from the plant's seed heads on dry, windy days. Often, the seeds travel no farther than 2 to 2.4 inches (5 to 6.1 centimeters) away from the adult plant.

Habitat and current distribution

The largest natural population of Robbins' cinquefoil is found on the Monroe Flats southwest of Mount Washington in the White Mountains in New Hampshire. There is another natural population located in the Franconia Mountains around 20 miles (32 kilometers) southwest of the Monroe Flats. According to the U.S. Fish and Wildlife Service (USFWS), prior to receiving Endangered Species Act (ESA) protection in 1980, the population of Robbins' cinquefoil was estimated at about 3,700 plants. In the summer of 2002, however, after a very successful recovery program, the population totaled more than 14,000 plants.

This species of cinquefoil inhabits sandy or rocky soil in harsh, barren mountainous areas of the White Mountain National Forest at an elevation of about 5,000 feet (1,524 meters). It prefers a southern exposure.

History and conservation measures

Because the Robbins' cinquefoil has such a limited range, any human disturbance of its habitat has had a devastating effect. As a result of collecting by plant enthusiasts and trampling by hikers, several original cinquefoil populations died out. In 1980, it was listed as an endangered species under ESA. In 1983, the White Mountain National Forest and the Appalachian Mountain Club (AMC) collaborated to reroute a hiking trail that lay in the remaining plants' critical habitat. They also put up fencing around the plants. The AMC used its resources to educate the public about the endangered plant and to collect seeds and help in transplanting it to suitable nearby areas. Another private organization, the New England Flower Society, participated with research and provided additional plants that it had propagated (caused to reproduce). Through the efforts of the government and these private organizations, new populations of Robbins' cinquefoil were able to thrive. From the brink of extinction, the species has recovered.

The recovery of the Robbins' cinquefoil was apparent in 1998, when the USFWS proposed to downgrade the species to threatened. On August 27, 2002, the species was removed entirely from the ESA list of threatened or endangered species. It has also been removed from the International Union for the Conservation of Nature and Natural Resources Red List of endangered species. The USFWS will continue to monitor the species for five years. The species will continue to be protected for many years to come under an agreement between the USFWS and the White Mountains National Forest.

CRESS, BRAUN'S ROCK
Arabis perstellata

DIVISION: Magnoliophyta
CLASS: Magnoliopsida
ORDER: Capparales
FAMILY: Brassicaceae
STATUS: Endangered, ESA
RANGE: USA (Kentucky, Tennessee)

Cress, Braun's rock

Arabis perstellata

Description and biology

Braun's rock cress is a member of the mustard family. There are two varieties of the species, the *Arabis perstellata* var. *ampla*, and *Arabis perstellata* var. *perstellata*. Braun's rock cress is a perennial (plant that lives, grows, flowers, and produces seeds for three or more consecutive years) that forms a low mat with gray foliage (leaves) and white–to–lavender flowers. There is downy hair on both its stem and its foliage. The plant's stem can grow to about 32 inches (80 centimeters) long. The plant produces a new cluster of leaves at its base annually. New branches grow from the leaf cluster produced the prior year. Lower leaves range in size from 1.6 to 6 inches (4 to 15 centimeters). Upper leaves measure only about 1.4 inches (3.5 centimeters). The flowers have four tiny petals and four pale green sepals (a kind of leaf at the base of the flower petals). Braun's rock cress produces flowers from late March to early May and mature fruits in mid–May to early June. Its

seeds are reddish brown and only about 0.04 inches (1 millimeter) long.

Habitat and current distribution

Braun's rock cress grows on moist, but not usually wet, rocky formations protruding from steep, wooded slopes. They also occur around the bases of trees. They live in full shade or filtered light.

One subspecies, the small rock cress (*Arabis p.* var.*perstellata*), occurs in 27 populations in Kentucky, mainly in Franklin County, but with a few in Owen and Henry Counties. The other subspecies, the large rock cress (*Arabis p.* var. *ampla*) is known to exist only in two populations in Rutherford County, Tennessee.

History and conservation measures

The surviving populations of Braun's rock cress are threatened by the destruction of their natural habitat, by the introduction of weeds that compete for their space, by livestock trampling them, by logging, and by construction. There are about 10 populations of the small rock cress that have not at this time been threatened by any of these conditions, but are likely to be threatened in the near future as development progresses. One of the two populations of the large rock cress consists of older plants, suggesting that the plants have not been reproducing.

The populations of Braun's rock cress in Kentucky occur on privately owned land. The Kentucky Nature Preserves Commission has worked with the landowners to try to protect the species within its natural habitat. In 2001, one of the landowners enrolled a 118–acre parcel of land—the natural habitat of Braun's rock cress—on the Kentucky Natural Areas Registry program, to be preserved as a natural area. While the private owners and the state have been striving to save the species, critics have claimed that the U.S. Fish and Wildlife Service (USFWS) has not fulfilled its obligations to the species under the Endangered Species Act (ESA). On November 8, 2001, a federal judge ordered the USFWS to designate critical habitat for 16 endangered species. One of these 16 endangered species was Braun's rock cress. Although the species had been designated as endangered, there had been no attempt to preserve habitat for it, as required under the ESA. In 2003, the USFWS responded to the court case, saying that designating critical habitat for endangered species as required by the ESA was slowing down its processes and distracting the agency from more important species protection.

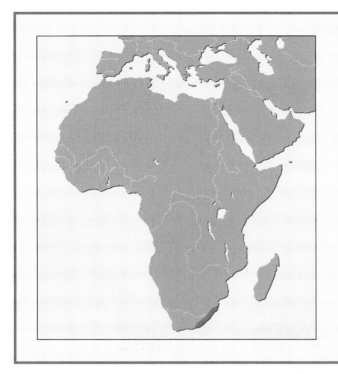

CYCAD, NATAL GRASS
Stangeria eriopus

DIVISION: Pinophyta
CLASS: Cycadopsida
ORDER: Cycadales
FAMILY: Stangeriaceae
STATUS: Rare, IUCN
RANGE: South Africa

Cycad, Natal grass

Stangeria eriopus

Description and biology

The Natal grass cycad is a palmlike perennial (plant that lives, grows, flowers, and produces seeds for three or more consecutive years). It grows to about 12 inches (30 centimeters) above the ground. Its underground stem may branch into several new stems. Up to four leaves grow from each of these growing points.

The plant's leaves measure from 1.5 to 6.5 feet (0.5 to 2 meters) long. Each leaf contains numerous leaflets that measure 4 to 16 inches (10 to 41 centimeters) long. The size and shape of the leaflets vary depending on the habitat. The leaflets of plants growing in open grassland are erect and compact, and have smooth margins or edges. Those of plants growing in forested habitats are taller and have serrated or saw–toothed margins.

The Natal grass cycad is dioecious (pronounced die–O–shus). This means that one cycad will have male cones while another will have female cones. The male cones, which give off pollen, are 4 to 6 inches (10 to 15 centimeters) long and 1 to 2 inches (2.5 to 5 centimeters) in diameter. Female cones, which bear seeds after having been pollinated, are 7 to 8 inches (18 to 20 centimeters) long and 3 to 4 inches (8 to 10 centimeters) in diameter. Female cones bear 80 to 100 seeds.

Habitat and current distribution

This species of cycad is unique to the eastern coastal areas of South Africa. It is found both in coastal grasslands (where it grows in full sun) and in inland evergreen forests within 31 miles (50 kilometers) of the ocean (where it grows in semi–shade). Those plants growing in full sun produce more cones than those growing in the shade.

Botanists (people specializing in the study of plants) are unsure of the total number of plants currently in existence, but they estimate that more than 50,000 are gathered each year for the herbal trade in Natal (eastern province in South Africa).

History and conservation measures

The Natal grass cycad was first identified in 1853. Since then, it has been popular with collectors and in botanical gardens worldwide. The primary threat to this species today is overcollecting for magical and medicinal purposes.

Native people in the cycad's range steep the plant in hot water to create a liquid extract or tea. They then sprinkle the liquid extract around their homes, believing it helps ward off lightning and evil spirits. They also give the liquid to infants suffering from congestion. Chemical studies of the Natal grass cycad, however, have not found any medicinal properties.

The Natal grass cycad is protected by international treaties. In all South African provinces, it is listed as a Specially Protected Plant. In order to meet the increasing demand for the plant as an herbal remedy, attempts are being made to breed the cycad artificially on a large scale.

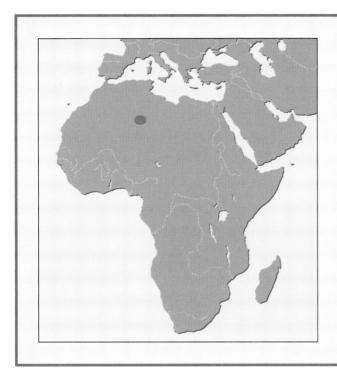

CYPRESS, SAHARAN
Cupressus dupreziana

DIVISION: Pinophyta

CLASS: Pinopsida

ORDER: Coniferales

FAMILY: Cupressaceae

STATUS: Critically endangered, IUCN

RANGE: Algeria

Cypress, Saharan

Cupressus dupreziana

Description and biology

Cypresses are resinous (containing a substance used in varnishes and lacquers) evergreens that have fragrant, durable wood. The true cypresses, of the genus *Cupressus,* are found in southern Europe, the Far East, and western North America.

A true cypress, the Saharan cypress, is covered in reddish–brown bark containing many deep cracks. It can grow to a height of 66 feet (20 meters) and a diameter of 13 feet (4 meters). It has upward–curving branches with flattened branchlets that grow in two opposite rows. Its dense foliage consists of small green leaves measuring 0.04 to 0.06 inch (0.1 to 0.15 centimeter) long. The tree's small cones are yellow or gray–brown.

Saharan cypresses can live for more than 1,000 years.

Habitat and current distribution

This cypress species is found in Algeria on the Tassili Plateau in the central Sahara Desert. In the late 1970s, botanists (people specializing in the study of plants) estimated that 150 adult cypresses existed in this area. In the early 2000s, botanists have estimated the population at 153 individual plants; there are only three populations of this species.

The Saharan cypress inhabits sandstone or gravel areas where the average annual rainfall is just 0.7 inch (1.8 centimeters). It grows in the bottom of usually dry streambeds or valleys where water sometimes collects. In this way, it takes advantage of any moisture that falls on the area.

History and conservation measures

Over thousands of years, humans have cut down innumerable cypresses for their long–lasting timber. The gates of St. Peter's in Rome, which stood for 1,100 years, were made of Italian cypresses (*Cupressus sempervirens*). Today, the cypress is a symbol of immortality for many people.

Saharan cypresses are critically endangered because they do not reproduce very quickly, and humans have cut them down before they have had the chance. Most of the surviving trees are just over 100 years old. Grazing animals have also destroyed many cypress seedlings before they have had a chance to root and grow.

At the end of the twentieth century, it appeared that if remaining habitats were protected, then the Saharan cypress might have a chance of survival. In the early 2000s, however, the International Union for the Conservation of Nature and Natural Resources (IUCN) upgraded the species from endangered to critically endangered because a low water table in the Sahara has further impeded reproduction of the Saharan cypress.

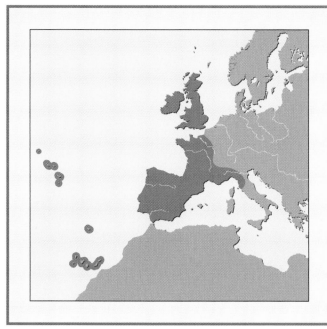

FERN, BRISTLE
Trichomanes speciosum

DIVISION: Polypodiophyta
CLASS: Polypodiopsida
ORDER: Filicales
FAMILY: Hymenophylaceae
STATUS: Rare, IUCN
RANGE: Azores, Canary Islands, France, Ireland, Italy, Madeira, Portugal, Spain, United Kingdom

Fern, bristle

Trichomanes speciosum

Description and biology

The bristle fern has thin, very dry, egg–shaped leaves that measure about 4 to 16 inches long. The leaves are attached to creeping, wiry stems. As the plant matures, structures at the margins (edges) of the leaves harden to form a bristle (point), thus giving the plant its common name.

Ferns reproduce by dispersing spores (tiny, usually one–celled reproductive bodies) instead of seeds. The spore cases, called sporangia (pronounced spor–AN–ja), are located in pockets on the margins of the leaves. Botanists (people specializing in the study of plants) believe the green spores of the bristle fern are dispersed by water (rain and other precipitation) rather than wind.

Habitat and current distribution

The bristle fern is considered vulnerable throughout most of its range. In France and Portugal, it is endangered. The

The bristle fern needs a constant source of flowing water. Because the plant has very thin leaves, it is most often found in dark crevices and gullies in deep, narrow, wooded valleys in areas where rainfall is plentiful.

plant is faring better in Ireland and Spain, where it is listed as rare.

The bristle fern needs a constant source of flowing water. Because the plant has very thin leaves, it is most often found in dark crevices and gullies in deep, narrow, wooded valleys in areas where rainfall is plentiful. It is also found growing in sandstone close to streams and waterfalls.

History and conservation measures

In the nineteenth century, this fern species was sought after to adorn sitting rooms in England and other European countries. Because of its decorative nature, the plant is still quite popular and is commonly grown in botanical gardens.

In the wild, the bristle fern is threatened throughout its range by deforestation (clearing away trees from a forest). In a number of areas in northern Spain, it is also threatened by spreading eucalyptus plantations.

Although the bristle fern is protected under the Bern Convention and the European Union Habitats Directive, no other conservation measures have currently been established.

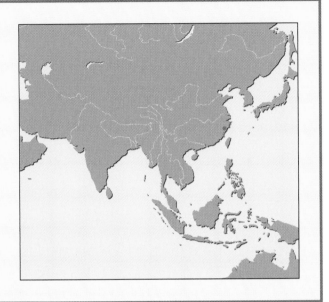

Fir, Baishan

Abies beshanzuensis

Description and biology

The Baishan fir is an evergreen tree with spreading, whorled branches (whorled means that three or more branches grow from the same area of trunk in a circular pattern). Its bark is grayish–yellow. The tree can grow to a height of 56 feet (17 meters). Annual shoots (new stem and leaf growth) are pale yellow or gray–yellow in color and smooth. The leaves on the tree measure 0.4 to 1.7 inches (1 to 4.3 centimeters) long and 0.1 to 0.14 inch (0.25 to 0.36 centimeter) wide. Its cones are pale brown or brownish–yellow when mature. They measure 2.8 to 4.7 inches (7.1 to 11.9 centimeters) long and 1.4 to 1.6 inches (3.6 to 4.1 centimeters) wide. The cones ripen or open and shed their seeds in November.

Habitat and current distribution

Baishan firs are found only in southeastern China. They inhabit the sunny forest slopes of Baishanzu Mountain in southern Zhejiang Province. They grow at an elevation of

5,577 feet (1,700 meters), where the climate is marked by warm summers and cool, moist winters.

Currently, botanists (people specializing in the study of plants) know of only five living specimens of these firs in the wild.

History and conservation measures

The remaining Baishan firs are growing in an area where local farmers are constantly employing slash–and–burn agriculture. In this process, farmers cut down and burn all trees and vegetation in a forest to create cleared land. Although this technique opens up the land quickly, it robs the soil of essential nutrients. The land does not stay fertile for very long. Thus, farmers must continually clear new land in order to grow crops.

Baishan firs have suffered as a result of this farming method. Most have been either cut down or burned. Those that remain cannot reproduce very well because the surrounding soil is not fertile enough.

The local forestry department in Zhejiang Province has granted the Baishan fir a limited degree of protection. If the species is to survive, greater protection is necessary.

**FORGET–ME–NOT,
CHATHAM ISLANDS**
Myosotidium hortensia

DIVISION: Magnoliophyta
CLASS: Magnoliopsida
ORDER: Asterales
FAMILY: Boraginaceae
STATUS: Rare, IUCN
RANGE: New Zealand
(Chatham Islands)

Forget-me-not, Chatham Islands

Myosotidium hortensia

Description and biology

The Chatham Islands forget–me–not is classified as a perennial (plant that lives, grows, flowers, and produces seeds for three or more consecutive years). It is also a succulent, or a plant that has thick, fleshy, water–storing leaves or stems. Its stout, fleshy underground stem produces a rosette, or crowded cluster of large leaves that form the plant's base. Measuring 6 to 17 inches (15 to 43 centimeters) long, the leaves are heart–shaped, thick, and fleshy.

Flowering stems arise from the plant's rosette to a height of 3.3 feet (1 meter). Attached to the stems are clusters of flowers that are pale to dark blue in color. Each flower is saucer–shaped and measures about 0.5 inch (1.3 centimeters) across.

Habitat and current distribution

The Chatham Islands forget–me–not is found on Chatham Islands, a island group lying about 500 miles (805 kilometers) east of New Zealand (to which it belongs). The plant is found on both main islands—Chatham and Pitt Islands—and on the islets (small islands) comprising the group.

Always found close to the sea, the Chatham Islands forget–me–not inhabits coastal dunes, sandy beaches, cliff ledges, and peat–covered rocks.

History and conservation measures

This species of forget–me–not was once plentiful throughout the Chatham Islands. It covered many acres of shoreline just above the high–water mark and spread farther inland over the sand dunes.

The plant has disappeared from much of its former range because of grazing by introduced animals. Pigs, sheep, and goats brought to the islands feed on the forget–me–not's leaves and stout, fleshy stems.

Two of the small islets in the Chatham Islands are nature reserves, and the Chatham Islands forget–me–not is slowly making a comeback at these locations. Fortunately, this plant is easy to grow from seeds; it is being artificially raised in great numbers.

GOLDENROD, SHORT'S
Solidago shortii

DIVISION: Magnoliophyta
CLASS: Magnoliopsida
ORDER: Asterales
FAMILY: Asteraceae
STATUS: Endangered, ESA
RANGE: USA (Kentucky)

Goldenrod, Short's

Solidago shortii

Description and biology

Short's goldenrod is an herb that grows to 24 to 30 inches (61 to 76 centimeters) high. It is classified as a perennial (plant that lives, grows, flowers, and produces seeds for three or more consecutive years). During the growing season, its underground stem may produce as many as six other separate stems that will create new plants.

The plant's leaves grow along the stem alternately (each leaf is attached to the stem on the side opposite to that of the leaf growing immediately above and below it). The leaves are narrow, measuring 2 to 4 inches (5 to 10 centimeters) long and 0.2 to 0.6 inch (0.5 to 1.5 centimeters) wide. Those leaves growing near the middle of the stem are larger than those growing toward each end.

The goldenrod's yellow flowers, which are gathered in clusters of ten or more, bloom from mid–August to early

November. Seeds are released from late September to late November. Botanists (people specializing in the study of plants) believe the sweat bee and other insects pollinate the plant when they seek out the flowers' nectar.

Habitat and current distribution

This species of goldenrod is unique to Kentucky. Five populations exist, the largest of which lies within Blue Licks Battlefield State Park. The other four populations are within a 2–mile (3.2–kilometer) radius of the park. Botanists estimate the total population to be between 3,400 and 4,000 individual plants.

Short's goldenrod inhabits cedar glades, pastures, and open areas in oak and hickory forests.

History and conservation measures

Short's goldenrod was first identified in 1842 in a site near the Ohio River in Jefferson County, Kentucky. All plants at that site were later destroyed when the site was flooded as a result of dam construction.

The primary threat to Short's goldenrod is the loss of its habitat due to human activities and fire (both man–made and natural). Overcollection by scientists is an additional threat.

Part of the Blue Licks Battlefield State Park has been designated a nature reserve to protect Short's goldenrod. Most remaining populations are on private land. To ensure the survival of this plant species, it is necessary that private landowners cooperate with any conservation measures.

DID YOU KNOW?

Short's goldenrod was originally found in 1840 by Charles Short, a Kentucky physician and botanist (person specializing in the study of plants). His discovery was new to science, and in 1842 the plant was given the scientific name *Solidago shortii* in his honor. Short found the goldenrod at the Falls on Rock Island, a rocky promontory (a ridge of land jutting out into a body of water) in the Kentucky portion of the Falls of the Ohio. Since that time, the promontory and the plants Short discovered there have been destroyed.

MAHOGANY, AMERICAN
Swietenia mahagoni

DIVISION: Tracheophyta
CLASS: Magnoliopsida
ORDER: Sapindales
FAMILY: Meliceae
STATUS: Endangered, IUCN
RANGE: Anguilla, Antigua and Barbuda, Bahamas, Barbados, Cayman Islands, Colombia, Cuba, Dominica, Dominican Republic, Grenada, Guadeloupe (Guadeloupe; St. Martin–St. Barthelemy), Jamaica, Martinique, Montserrat, Saint Kitts and Nevis, Saint Lucia, Saint Vincent and the Grenadines, Trinidad and Tobago, Turks and Caicos Islands, United States (Florida)

Mahogany, American
Swietenia mahagoni

Description and biology

The American mahogany, also called the West Indian or Cuban mahogany, is a fast–growing semi–evergreen tree. It grows to a height of about 40 to 60 feet (12.2 to 18.2 meters) and spreads out to a width of about the same measure. Its bark is smooth and gray in its early years and becomes darker and browner as the tree ages. An older tree has flaky, ridged bark. The 4– to 8–inch (10.2– to 20.5–centimeter) leaves come in clusters, with 4 to 8 leaflets of about one–quarter inch (.65 centimeter) length. The oval leaves are dark green on top and reddish–brown underneath. They have sharp tips and a smooth surface.

The American mahogany has small 3– to 6–inch green or white flowers that are barely noticeable to a casual observer.

632

The flowers are unisexual (either male or female, but not both, as some flowers are). They are pollinated by insects. In the fall or the winter, one flower will develop into a fruit, a large, woody, 2– to 5–inch (5– to 12–centimeter) pod. When the pods are mature (in 8 to 10 months), they release flat, brown seeds. This cycle usually takes place on an annual basis in trees that are 10 to 15 years old.

Few stands of American mahogany now exist in the wild because of the overexploitation of the species for the furniture industry and because of the development of the lands that the tree favors.

Habitat and current distribution

The American mahogany occurs in subtropical dry or wet forests at altitudes ranging from sea level to about 2,625 feet (800 meters). The species does best in rich, moist soil, but it is currently found most frequently in dry, stony areas. American mahogany trees are usually found scattered, with only one or two trees on a one–acre section of the forest.

The American mahogany is native to Cuba, Haiti, Jamaica, the Dominican Republic, the Bahamas, and the Florida Keys. The species, though, has been cultivated by humans for many years; in some cases it is difficult for scientists to determine which populations are native to an area. The species has been introduced to Puerto Rico, the Virgin Islands, the Lesser Antilles, Trinidad, Tobago, and elsewhere in the Caribbean Islands.

History and conservation measures

American mahogany has long been prized for its durable, deep red, straight–grained wood, which has been used to make fine furniture for centuries. It was first used during the reign of King George I of England (1714 to 1727). Europe imported its mahogany from Jamaica, Cuba, and Honduras. By 1774, American mahogany had become scarce because of its popularity in furniture–making. By the late 1800s, the species was nearly eliminated from Cuba, and was in decline elsewhere.

Few stands of American mahogany now exist in the wild because of the overexploitation of the species for the furniture industry and because of the development of the lands that the tree favors. The species is much more likely to be found planted in someone's yard or along a city street than in its natural habitat. Where it does grow wild, the species has undergone dramatic changes. Trees are likely to be much smaller and more like bushes, with many branches.

Since 1992, the trade of American mahogany has been restricted under the Convention on International Trade in Endangered Species of Wild Fauna and Flora (CITES). It has an Appendix II listing under CITES, which means that an exporter of this wood must receive a permit from the government. Trade in the species is now often in salvaged wood.

ORCHID, EASTERN PRAIRIE FRINGED
Platanthera leucophaea

DIVISION: Magnoliophyta
CLASS: Liliopsida
ORDER: Orchidales
FAMILY: Orchidaceae
STATUS: Threatened, ESA
RANGE: Canada, USA

Orchid, eastern prairie fringed

Platanthera leucophaea

Description and biology

The eastern prairie fringed orchid is considered one of the most beautiful plants in North America. It is classified as a perennial (plant that lives, grows, flowers, and produces seeds for three or more consecutive years). After lying dormant all winter, the plant finally sends up leaves and a flower spike in June. Depending on the amount of moisture that has fallen during the season, this stout orchid can grow to a height of almost 40 inches (102 centimeters).

The orchid's stem is angled and leafy. The silver–green leaves grow along the stem alternately (each leaf is attached to the stem on the side opposite to that of the leaf growing immediately above and below it). They measure 3 to 8 inches (7.6 to 20 centimeters) long and 1 to 2 inches (2.5 to 5

centimeters) wide. The two lowermost leaves on the stem are larger than the rest.

Ten to forty white flowers grow off the stem. These showy flowers have a deeply fringed three–part lower lip, which gives the plant its common name. At night, the flowers release a scent to attract nocturnal (active at night) hawkmoths to help pollinate the plant.

Eastern prairie fringed orchids can be long–lived. Individual plants have been known to survive more than 30 years.

Habitat and current distribution

The eastern prairie fringed orchid is currently found in the Canadian provinces of Nova Scotia and Ontario and in seven U.S. states: Illinois, Iowa, Maine, Michigan, Ohio, Virginia, and Wisconsin. The plant is considered rare in its Canadian range. In the United States, very small populations occur in Iowa, Maine, Ohio, and Virginia. Larger populations are found in Illinois and Wisconsin. Michigan contains the greatest concentration of eastern prairie fringed orchids. In the mid–1980s, botanists (people specializing in the study of plants) estimated that 18 populations with more than 1,300 individual plants existed in the state.

The eastern prairie fringed orchid commonly grows in full sunlight on the rich, moist, and sandy soils of open prairies. It also grows on sedge mats in open bogs, areas of wet spongy ground composed chiefly of decomposed sedge plant matter. In Michigan, it is often found growing on tufts of sedge or grass or on logs in lakes.

History and conservation measures

The main reason for the decline of this orchid species is habitat destruction. The fertile, moist soil in which the plant grows is prized by farmers, and much of its prairie land habitat has been converted into farmland. This process still poses a threat to some surviving orchid populations.

None of the known eastern prairie fringed orchid populations inhabit federally protected land. However, certain populations receive state protection in Illinois, Michigan, and Wisconsin.

DIVISION: Magnoliophyta
CLASS: Liliopsida
ORDER: Arecales
FAMILY: Arecaceae
STATUS: Critically endangered, IUCN
RANGE: Egypt, Sudan

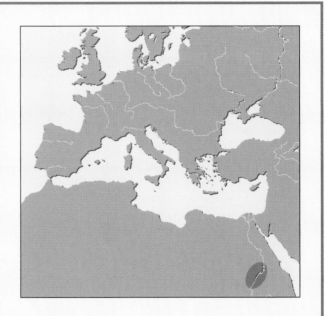

Palm, Argun

Medemia argun

Description and biology

The Argun palm can grow to a height of almost 33 feet (10 meters). Its bare trunk sprouts no branches, but is topped by a crown of leaves. These fan–shaped leaves measure up to 4.4 feet (1.3 meters) long. Each compound leaf (called a frond) is composed of numerous stiff, sword–shaped leaflets, which measure 0.4 to 1.6 inches (1 to 4 centimeters) wide. These leaflets grow opposite each other on either side of the leaf's stalk or rachis (pronounced RAY–kiss).

This palm is dioecious (pronounced die–O–shus). This means that one Argun palm will have male flowers (which give off pollen) while another will have female flowers (which receive the pollen). The male flowers are small with three spreading petals. They are attached to the palm by dense spikes that measure 6 to 11 inches (15 to 28 centimeters) in length. The female flowers are rounded and measure approximately 0.2 inch (0.5 centimeter) across. They are attached to stout stalks 0.4 inch (1 centimeter) long that protrude from similar spikes.

Habitat and current distribution

The Argun palm has been found only in a few sites in Egypt and Sudan. In the early 1960s, botanists (people specializing in the study of plants) found one tree in an uninhabited oasis (fertile area in a desert) 140 miles (225 kilometers) southwest of the Egyptian city of Aswan. Another single palm was found in a similar site about 125 miles (200 kilometers) west of Aswan. A final group of palms was discovered on the east side of the Nile River in the south. In Sudan, some palms were found at a site 125 miles (200 kilometers) southeast of the city of Wadi Halfa in the northern region of the country.

In the mid 1990s, botanists were unable to find any live Argun palms and began to believe that the species was extinct. In 1995, however, several small, fragmented populations of the species were found in Sudan. It appears that these populations are able to reproduce.

The Argun palm is found in groves on river banks and in oases or wadis (stream beds or valleys that are usually dry except during the rainy season).

History and conservation measures

In ancient Egypt, the Argun palm was widespread and was placed as an offering in tombs.

Now, the Argun palm is among the most threatened of any palm species in the world. It has been cut down in great numbers because native people in its range use its leaves to make mats. Much of its natural habitat also has been destroyed by irrigation projects along the Nile River that feed water to farms.

Since the 1995 discovery of Argun palms in Sudan, botanists (people specializing in the study of plants) have been collecting the seeds of the plants for cultivation.

PALM, CAROSSIER
Attalea crassispatha

DIVISION: Magnoliophyta

CLASS: Liliopsida

ORDER: Arecales

FAMILY: Arececeae

STATUS: Critically endangered, IUCN

RANGE: Haiti

Palm, carossier
Attalea crassispatha

Description and biology

The carossier palm, or *petit coco* (little coconut), is a tall, solitary palm that grows to a height of 65 feet (20 meters). Its smooth gray trunk measures up to 13.8 inches (35 centimeters) in diameter. It has a crown of 15 to 19 arching leaves that measure up to 17.5 feet (5.3 meters) long. Each compound leaf (called a frond) is composed of numerous smooth–edged leaflets. These leaflets grow opposite each other at regular spaces on either side of the leaf's stalk, or rachis (pronounced RAY–kiss).

This palm produces fruits that resemble tiny coconuts (hence the palm's common name on Haiti). Each fruit consists of a fibrous, hard shell surrounding a small, white, hollow kernel that is edible. The fruits are egg–shaped and taper to a sharp point. They measure 1.25 to 1.75 inches (3.18 to 4.45 centimeters) in length. When mature (ripe), they are reddish in color.

Habitat and current distribution

The carossier palm is found only on Haiti's southwestern peninsula, an area once dominated by tropical scrub (stunted trees or shrubs) vegetation. In the late 1980s, botanists (people specializing in the study of plants) located 26 palms of various ages in 5 small populations. All of these surviving wild palms are on private lands. In 1996, fewer than 30 individual plants were found on Haiti.

This palm prefers to grow in full sunlight at or near sea level.

History and conservation measures

The carossier palm was first described in 1689 by a French priest and naturalist. He wrote that the palm was abundant in southwestern Haiti. By the 1920s, when botanists first began to study the plant, it had begun to disappear and was considered a rarity. Botanists are deeply interested in the carossier palm because it is the only one of its genus (*Attalea*) that grows in the Caribbean.

Because of Haiti's growing human population and poor economy, many of the island's natural resources have been depleted. The carossier palm has been crowded out of its habitat by farming and its edible seeds have been collected by local people. Since the carossier palm is not currently growing in any protected areas, the outlook for its future is grim.

PINE, BIGCONE PINYON
Pinus maximartinezii

DIVISION: Pinophyta
CLASS: Pinopsida
ORDER: Coniferales
FAMILY: Pinaceae
STATUS: Endangered, IUCN
RANGE: Mexico

Pine, bigcone pinyon
Pinus maximartinezii

Description and biology

The bigcone pinyon pine is a small, busy tree with a short trunk that is often contorted. It has widely spreading branches. They are spaced irregularly along the trunk and form an open, rounded crown. The tree normally grows to a height between 16.4 and 32.8 feet (5 and 10 meters), although some have grown as high as 49 feet (15 meters). Its trunk measures up to 19.7 inches (50 centimeters) in diameter.

The bark of the bigcone pinyon pine is dark brown in color and is broken into square plates measuring almost 4 inches (10 centimeters) in diameter. The needles usually grow in clusters of five. They are slender and flexible, and measure 3.2 to 3.9 inches (8 to 10 centimeters) long. The needles on most bigcone pinyon pines are covered with a removable waxy coating that gives them a whitish or bluish cast.

The most remarkable feature about this pine is its huge cones (hence its common name). Among the largest and heaviest pinecones, they measure from 5.9 to 9.9 inches (15 to 25 centimeters) long and 3.9 to 5.9 inches (10 to 15 centimeters) wide. The cones are covered in thick, woody scales that often curve down or backward. The cones contain wingless, edible seeds measuring almost 1 inch in length and 0.5 inch in width. Again, these seeds are among the largest pine seeds. The cones, which take about two years to ripen, hang from the branches like woody pineapples.

Habitat and current distribution

Bigcone pinyon pines are found in only one area in Mexico, near the village of Pueblo Viejo in southern Zacatecas. This village lies about 62 miles (100 kilometers) north–northeast of the city of Guadalajara. The trees occupy a range of 1.9 to 3.9 square miles (5 to 10 square kilometers) on the eastern flanks of a mountain range called Sierra de Monroe. In this area, the pines grow on dry, rocky ground. Botanists (people specializing in the study of plants) estimate that between 3,000 and 10,000 bigcone pinyon pines currently exist in this area.

History and conservation measures

This species of pine was first scientifically identified in 1964. Prior to this discovery, local inhabitants in the tree's range had been harvesting its seeds for many years. Although the seeds are a minor food source of people in the area, the gathering of seeds is not extensive. Many cones are left on the trees.

Fire is the main threat to the bigcone pinyon pine since the tree regenerates, or reproduces, slowly. Fires are frequent in this area, as farmers burn vegetation to clear land for crops. In 1986, an extensive fire devastated a large area, burning mature trees, seedlings, and saplings. No part of the bigcone pinyon pine's range is currently under protection.

PITCHER PLANT, GREEN
Sarracenia oreophila

DIVISION: Magnoliophyta
CLASS: Magnoliopsida
ORDER: Dilleniales
FAMILY: Sarraceniaceae
STATUS: Critically endangered, IUCN
Endangered, ESA
RANGE: USA (Alabama and Georgia)

Pitcher plant, green

Sarracenia oreophila

Description and biology

The green pitcher plant is classified as a perennial (plant that lives, grows, flowers, and produces seeds for three or more consecutive years). It is insectivorous (pronounced in–sec–TIV–res), meaning it depends on insects for food.

The plant's green or yellow–green leaves grow to a height of 8 to 29.5 inches (20 to 75 centimeters). Wider at the top than at the bottom, the leaves resemble pitchers or horn–shaped enclosures. The pitcher–shaped leaves usually contain a sweet–smelling liquid. Insects are drawn to the liquid or to the plant's bright coloration. Once the insect enters the leaf, it is prevented from escaping by bristles on the inside of the leaf surface. Eventually, the insect drowns in the liquid. It is then broken down by enzymes (chemical compounds composed of proteins) and digested by the plant.

The leaves and flower buds appear in early April. The leaves mature and yellow flowers bloom during late April and

May. The pitcher–shaped leaves wither by late summer and are replaced by flat leaves that remain until the following spring.

A green pitcher plant with flowers. Insects, which make up the plants' diet, are often drawn to the plants' bright colors.

Habitat and current distribution

The green pitcher plant is found in only a few areas in Alabama and Georgia. The largest populations occupy the Cumberland Plateau region in Alabama. Botanists (people specializing in the study of plants) estimate that about 26 green pitcher plant populations exist in the wild. The size of these populations varies from a single plant to more than 1,000 plants.

Green pitcher plants require very acidic soil in which to grow. They are found in a variety of habitats (mainly wetland areas). These include bogs (areas of wet spongy ground composed of decaying plant matter), woodland sites that have poor drainage in winter, and sloping stream banks.

History and conservation measures

The green pitcher plant was never common, but it was found over a wider range than it is now. At one time, its range extended into Tennessee.

The decline of this plant is mainly due to the draining of its wetland habitat. The green pitcher plant is further threatened by herbicide and fertilizer runoff from farms in its range. Collectors who prize the unusual–looking plant have also reduced its numbers in the wild.

The survival of the green pitcher plant can be assured only if wetlands that form the base of its habitat are preserved.

POGONIA, SMALL WHORLED
Isotria medeoloides

DIVISION: Magnoliophyta
CLASS: Liliopsida
ORDER: Liliales
FAMILY: Orchidaceae
STATUS: Threatened, ESA
RANGE: Canada, USA

Pogonia, small whorled
Isotria medeoloides

Description and biology

The small whorled pogonia is considered one of the rarest orchids in eastern North America. It is classified as a perennial (plant that lives, grows, flowers, and produces seeds for three or more consecutive years). It has a waxy, pale green or purplish stem that grows 3.5 to 10 inches (8.9 to 25.4 centimeters) high. The stem is topped by five or six drooping, dusty green leaves arranged in a whorl, or spiral (hence the plant's common name). Each leaf measures 0.8 to 3.3 inches (2 to 8.4 centimeters) in length.

Growing above the leaves are one or two yellowish–green flowers that bloom in May and June and then die very quickly. The sepals (leaflike external whorls lying below the petals of the flowers) are green and narrow, measuring up to 1 inch (25 centimeters) in length. The petals are lance–shaped.

Botanists (people specializing in the study of plants) believe this species of orchid does not depend on insects in order to

Botanists believe the small whorled pogonia does not depend on insects in order to pollinate, but is self–pollinating.

pollinate (transferring pollen to the female parts of flowers), but is self–pollinating.

Habitat and current distribution

In Canada, the small whorled pogonia is found in Ontario. In the United States, it is found in the following states: Connecticut, Delaware, Georgia, Illinois, Maine, Maryland, Massachusetts, Michigan, New Hampshire, New Jersey, New

York, North Carolina, Ohio, Pennsylvania, Rhode Island, South Carolina, Tennessee, Vermont, and Virginia. The largest populations are in Maine and New Hampshire. Botanists estimate that approximately 1,500 individual small whorled pogonias currently exist.

The plant prefers to inhabit dry, open forests dominated by deciduous (shedding) trees, where it grows in acidic soil.

History and conservation measures

The small whorled pogonia has decreased in number because of many factors. The destruction of its habitat to create land for residential and industrial areas has been the main threat to this species. Because of the plant's beauty and scientific value, it has also been overcollected by private collectors and scientists.

The status of the small whorled pogonia has improved. While it was previously considered endangered, it is now viewed as threatened. Continuing conservation efforts include protecting existing populations and, especially, habitat.

DID YOU KNOW?

In 1995, the New Hampshire chapter of the Nature Conservancy, a nonprofit environmental organization, purchased 170 acres (68 hectares) at Mount Teneriffe, near the town of Milton, for use as a wildlife preserve. Biologists (people who study living organisms) consider this site to be one of the five most significant sites for the small whorled pogonia in the world. Besides providing a safe habitat for the plant, the new preserve also provides a safe haven for a variety of birds and other rare plants. In addition to being open to the public, the preserve serves as a research area for university scientists and graduate students.

**RHODODENDRON,
CHAPMAN'S**
Rhododendron chapmanii

DIVISION: Magnoliophyta

CLASS: Magnoliopsida

ORDER: Dilleniales

FAMILY: Ericaceae

STATUS: Endangered, ESA

RANGE: USA (Florida)

Rhododendron, Chapman's

Rhododendron chapmanii

Description and biology

Chapman's rhododendron is an evergreen shrub that can reach 6.6 feet (2 meters) high. The bark on new shoots is reddish–brown. As the plant ages, the bark turns gray and starts to peel. The rhododendron's leaves are oval–shaped, measuring 1.2 to 2.6 inches (3 to 6.6 centimeters) in length. They are green on top, but reddish underneath because the surface is lined with flat red scales.

Tight clusters of flowers bloom in March and April. The flowers are often pink, but the color can vary in large populations. Each flower has five petals measuring 1.2 to 1.4 inches (3 to 3.6 centimeters) long. The petals spread out in a funnel shape and are slightly unequal in size (the lowest is the largest).

In the past, botanists (people specializing in the study of plants) believed the plant reproduced by spreading seeds. This

does not seem to be the case now, however. Most Chapman's rhododendrons seem to reproduce in the wild by resprouting from roots.

Habitat and current distribution

This species of rhododendron is found only in Florida. Three populations exist, the largest of which straddles Gadsden and Liberty Counties. This population covers 150 to 200 acres (60 to 80 hectares) and numbers around 500 individual plants. A population of several hundred plants is found in Gulf County. The last population, made up of fewer than 50 plants, exists in Clay County.

Chapman's rhododendrons require a habitat that has good drainage and that will not flood. They prefer light shade and sandy soil that contains abundant organic matter. They are usually found inhabiting areas between dry pine–turkey oak vegetation and moist titi (tree with leathery leaves and fragrant flowers) bogs.

History and conservation measures

Much of this plants' habitat has been destroyed by logging and by the clearing of areas to create pine plantations. Although Chapman's rhododendron does well when other plants around it are cleared away, too much disturbance of its habitat can be destructive to the plant. Because the plant is also attractive, it has been collected in great numbers by nursery operators and amateur gardeners.

Much of the remaining populations of Chapman's rhododendron are on private land. Enlisting the cooperation of landowners to preserve the plants' habitat is one conservation effort currently underway. Additional measures include regulating logging and other forestry practices that would further destroy its habitat.

Rosewood, Brazilian

Dalbergia nigra

Description and biology

The Brazilian rosewood, or jacaranda, is a tropical timber tree that grows to a height of 50 to 82 feet (15 to 25 meters). Because most of these trees have been logged, those with thick trunks are rarely found. The remaining rosewoods have trunks measuring just 1 to 1.3 feet (0.3 to 0.4 meter) in diameter.

The tree's bark is thin, gray, and rough. Its branches are dark and roundish, and they grow in a slightly zig–zag manner from the trunk. The compound leaves are divided into 12 to 18 leaflets, each one measuring up to 0.6 inch (1.5 centimeters) long and 0.3 inch (0.8 centimeter) wide.

Brazilian rosewoods flower in October and November. The pale, violet–scented flowers are about 0.35 inch (0.89 centimeters) long and are arranged in bunches on leafless shoots.

Habitat and current distribution

The Brazilian rosewood is found in the Atlantic coastal forests of Brazil. It grows in a range of climates from southern Bahia to Minas Gerais (Brazilian states). It is most frequently found inhabiting rolling or mountainous terrain that has relatively fertile soil. Current population figures are not available.

History and conservation measures

The Brazilian rosewood is one of Brazil's finest woods. It is highly prized for its valuable heartwood, the central nonliving wood in the trunk of the tree. The heartwood is purplish–black in color and is rather oily and fragrant—hence the common name of rosewood. The durable wood of the Brazilian rosewood has been used for decorative veneers, high-quality furniture, musical instruments, tools, and craft products.

Brazilian rosewoods grew in great numbers when European explorers first came to South America in the early sixteenth century. Once the Europeans realized the value of its wood, they began cutting down the rosewood and shipping it around the world. Other rosewoods were cut down simply to create plantations and farms. Still more were cleared to aid mining operations. This deforestation continued for over 300 years, finally reaching its peak in the twentieth century. At present, Brazilian rosewoods occupy just 5 percent of their former range.

Only a tiny portion of the remaining rosewood forests are protected in national parks and reserves. The export of rosewood logs has been banned in Brazil for 30 years. In 1992, the Brazilian rosewood was added to Appendix I of the Convention on International Trade in Endangered Species of Wild Fauna and Flora (CITES; an international treaty to protect wildlife). This act prohibited the trade of the tree between nations that had signed the treaty.

Despite these protective measures, the Brazilian rosewood remains threatened by those who cut it down illegally and sell it for high prices.

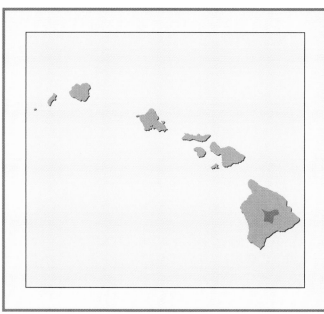

SILVERSWORD, KA'U
Argyroxiphium kauense

DIVISION: Magnoliophyta
CLASS: Magnoliopsida
ORDER: Asterales
FAMILY: Asteraceae
STATUS: Endangered, ESA
RANGE: USA (Hawaii)

Silversword, Ka'u

Argyroxiphium kauense

Description and biology

Ka'u (pronounced KAH–oo) silversword (also called Mauna Loa silversword) is a monocarpic plant (one that bears fruit and flower only once and then dies) of the aster family. It grows to a height ranging from 1 inch to 2 feet (3 to 70 centimeters) and has long flowering stems that grow from 2 to 8 feet (0.7 to 2.5 meters) long. The Ka'u silversword is a giant rosette (clustered) shrub with leaves covered with gray or silver hairs. The leaves are long and narrow, measuring about 8 to 16 inches in length and only about .2 inch (0.5 centimeters) in width. When the Ku'a silversword grows, its rosette widens in diameter and its stem gets taller. This growth occurs for several years before the plant produces a flowering stalk, called an inflorescence. The inflorescence has many branches, and each branch has a flowering head made up of 3 to 11 ray flowers that are about one-half inch (1 centimeter) long. Each of the ray flowers contains 50 to 200 florets that are only about 0.2 inch (0.6 cm) long. The flowers, which

range in color from white or yellow to deep red, bloom in August and September. The fruits the plant produces are dry and black. Once the fruit sets, the plant dies. Scientists believe that flying insects, probably native bees, pollinate the species.

Habitat and current distribution

The Ka'u silversword grows in moist open forest areas or bogs, generally at altitudes between 3,330 and 9,100 feet (1,625 and 2,774 meters). It also occurs in some dry areas in which smooth lava is covered by a shallow layer of soil. There are only three known populations of this species and they are on Mauna Loa, a large volcanic mountain on the island of Hawaii. They are located on private land on Kahuku Ranch and on state–owned land in the Upper Waiakea and Kapapala Forest Reserves. The population of the species in the wild has been estimated to be under 500 individual plants. There are an additional 1,000 individual plants that were planted at Kapapala and another 1,000 planted in Hawaii Volcanoes National Park.

History and conservation measures

At one time the Ka'u silversword probably existed across the island of Hawaii, in a band stretching from the southwest of the island to the northeast slope of Mauna Lao. It also probably existed on Hualalai. It is interesting to note that the plant is endemic (native to and occurring only in) to a volcanic mountain and has survived its lava flows with a healthy population for many years.

Today, because of its low population, the Ka'u silversword is extremely vulnerable to extinction. Browsing (feeding) animals are a particular threat. Cows and feral animals (once-tame animals that have escaped into the wild) such as pigs, goats, and mouflon sheep have greatly reduced its numbers and prevent it from recovery. The animals tend to eat older, more mature plants. Since the plant flowers only one time in its life, their browsing significantly reduces reproduction. With so few remaining plants, the gene pool (the number of units that pass on inherited traits) is quite low, which may weaken the species. Since there are only three surviving populations—and those three are located on a volcano—there is strong risk that lava flow or fire could entirely wipe out the species. Pests, drought, disease, and the introduction of alien species also threaten the Ka'u silversword.

Protective fencing has been built around existing populations of the species since the 1970s to keep feral animals from browsing and trampling the plants. Controlling the ungulates (hooved animals) around the Ka'u silversword habitat is crucial to its survival. Research into the effects of nonnative plants and habitat requirements is ongoing.

Torreya, Florida

Torreya taxifolia

Description and biology

The Florida torreya (pronounced too–REE–a) is a relatively small evergreen tree that usually grows to a height of 30 feet (9 meters). However, some torreyas grow as high as 59 feet (18 meters). Stiff, sharp–pointed needles grow along opposite sides of the branches, making them appear flattened. When crushed, the needles give off a strong resinous odor. Because of this, the tree is sometimes called the "stinking cedar."

The torreya is dioecious (pronounced die–O–shus). This means that one torreya will have male cones while another will have female cones. Male cones give off pollen in March and April. Over the course of the summer, the pollinated female cones develop into dark green, oval–shaped seeds 1 to 1.5 inches (2.5 to 3.8 centimeters) long. The seeds then drop off in the fall. The tree reaches maturity (and is thus able to give off pollen and seeds) after about 20 years.

Habitat and current distribution

Florida torreyas are found only in the Apalachicola River area in Gadsden, Liberty, and Jackson Counties in Florida and in a closely adjacent part of Decatur County, Georgia. The trees grow along the steep sides of ravines and on bluffs in the moist shade of pine and hardwood trees. The total number of these trees currently in existence is unknown.

History and conservation measures

The range of the Florida torreya has not changed over the years, but the number of trees within that range has dropped significantly. One reason for this drop was that many sections within the range were cleared to create residential areas. This is no longer a threat, as remaining habitat areas are not easily reached and are not suitable for housing.

The Florida torreya is sometimes called the "stinking cedar" because of the strong resinous odor its needles release.

The main threat currently facing the Florida torreya is disease. Beginning in the 1950s, a fungal disease attacked and killed most of the trees in the area. New trees resprouted from the old roots and stumps, but they also became infected and died long before reaching maturity.

Unless a solution can be found for the disease affecting the Florida torreya, it may soon become extinct in the wild.

TRILLIUM, RELICT
Trillium reliquum

DIVISION: Magnoliophyta
CLASS: Liliopsida
ORDER: Liliales
FAMILY: Liliaceae
STATUS: Endangered, ESA
RANGE: USA (Alabama, Georgia, South Carolina)

Trillium, relict
Trillium reliquum

Description and biology

Trilliums are attractive spring wildflowers that belong to the lily family. About half a dozen trillium species grace North American woodlands. All trilliums are classified as perennials (plants that live, grow, flower, and produce seeds for three or more consecutive years). These short, erect plants all have leaves and flowers in three parts.

The relict trillium differs from other species in its family in the shape of its slow S–curved stems. Its flowers, which bloom in early spring, range in color from yellow to green to brownish–purple. Bright red berries, technically called the plant's fruit, adorn the trillium each autumn. After the fruit matures, the plant dies back to its underground stem.

Habitat and current distribution

This trillium species is found in Alabama, Georgia, and South Carolina, where there are 21 known populations. The

largest single site, containing an estimated 50,000 to 100,000 individual plants, is in Aiken and Edgefield Counties in South Carolina.

The relict trillium prefers to inhabit mature, moist, undisturbed hardwood forests where the soil has a high organic content.

History and conservation measures

Logging, road construction, and the clearing of forests to create farms and residential areas have all combined to reduce the number of relict trilliums in existence. These factors continue to threaten remaining trillium habitat. The plant is also threatened by introduced plant species such as Japanese honeysuckle and kudzu, both weedy vines.

While some relict trillium habitat lies on protected land, most is on private land. Some landowners have agreed to cooperate in protecting the plant, but some populations are still at risk. Plans to introduce the relict trillium into protected areas are underway.

VENUS'S–FLYTRAP
Dionaea muscipula

DIVISION: Magnoliophyta
CLASS: Magnoliopsida
ORDER: Nepenthalesniales
FAMILY: Droseraceae
STATUS: Vulnerable, IUCN
RANGE: USA (North Carolina and South Carolina)

Venus's-flytrap

Dionaea muscipula

Description and biology

The Venus's–flytrap is one of North America's most well–known carnivorous or insectivorous plants. Insectivorous (pronounced in–sec–TIV–res) means that the plant depends on insects for food (it also preys on small animals). The Venus's–flytrap is classified as a perennial (plant that lives, grows, flowers, and produces seeds for three or more consecutive years).

The plant can grow to a height of about 12 inches (30.5 centimeters). It has 4 to 8 leaves, each measuring 0.8 to 4.7 inches (2 to 12 centimeters) in length. The leaves grow around the base of the plant, forming a rosette, or rounded cluster. The end of each leaf is divided into identical, semicircular halves that are connected or hinged at the midrib. The margins, or edges, of each half bear long, sharp spines.

The leaves secrete a sweet fluid, which attracts insects and small animals. When an insect lands on the leaf, it touches

A Venus's–flytrap readies itself to capture its prey. It is one of North America's most famous carnivorous plants.

trigger hairs at the center of the leaf. When touched, these hairs cause the leaf to snap shut around the prey. The spines interlock and the prey cannot escape. The plant then releases digestive solutions to dissolve the prey's body. After the prey is fully digested, the leaf reopens.

The Venus's–flytrap has a flowering stem that rises above the rosette. At the top of the stem is a cluster of 4 to 10 small, white flowers. Flowering begins near the last week in May and is usually over before the middle of June.

Habitat and current distribution

This plant is found on the coastal plain of North Carolina and South Carolina. Its range extends for about 200 miles (320 kilometers) from Beaufort County in North Carolina to Charleston County in South Carolina. Botanists (people specializing in the study of plants) are unsure of the total number of Venus's–flytraps currently in existence.

Venus's–flytrap prefers to inhabit open, sunny bogs (areas of wet, spongy ground composed of decaying plant matter). Because the soil in bogs is low in nitrogen, the plant derives that nutrient from the insects and small animals on which it feeds.

History and conservation measures

The Venus's–flytrap once existed in great numbers, but since the 1970s its populations have been small. The two main reasons for the plant's decline are habitat destruction and overcollection.

Fire plays an important role in the Venus's–flytrap's habitat. Frequent natural fires remove most of the low vegetation in the plant's area. When these fires are put out quickly or even prevented, the Venus's–flytrap faces competition from other plants and is often destroyed.

Another habitat threat is the draining of wetland areas to create land suitable for housing or farming. Any permanent drop in the water level of a site can destroy any and all Venus's–flytraps inhabiting it.

Even though laws protect the Venus's–flytrap in both North Carolina and South Carolina, collectors treasure the plant, and it is still collected illegally from the wild. In 1990, more than 1,100,000 plants were exported overseas from North Carolina. Of these, over 300,000 were wild species.

WILD RICE, TEXAS
Zizania texana

DIVISION: Magnoliophyta
CLASS: Liliopsida
ORDER: Cyperales
FAMILY: Gramineae
STATUS: Endangered, ESA
RANGE: USA (Texas)

Wild rice, Texas

Zizania texana

Description and biology

Texas wild rice is a coarse, aquatic grass with long, underwater stems. It is classified as a perennial (plant that lives, grows, flowers, and produces seeds for three or more consecutive years). Its leaves are green, thin, flat, and very long. They measure up to 45 inches (114 centimeters) long and 0.25 to 1 inch (0.64 to 2.54 centimeters) wide. The lower part of the grass, with leaves, often floats on the water. This part of the plant can measure 3.5 feet (1.1 meter) long.

Flower stalks, when present, extend 12 to 35 inches (30.5 to 89 centimeters) above the surface of the water. The plant flowers and produces grainlike seeds at various times from April to November. Texas wild rice is related to the wild rice plants that people eat, but it is not used for food.

Habitat and current distribution

This grass species is found only in a 1.5–mile (2.4–kilometer) length of the headwaters of the San Marcos River in south–central Texas.

Texas wild rice forms large clumps that are firmly rooted in the gravel bottom near the middle of the river. It prefers clear, cool, fast–flowing spring water. An increase of silt (mineral particles) in the water, the disturbance of the river's bottom, and stagnant water all will kill the plant.

History and conservation measures

Texas wild rice was first identified in 1933. At the time, it was abundant in the headwaters of the San Marcos River, in nearby irrigation ditches, and for about 1,000 feet (305

Habitat destruction is the main reason for the decline of the Texas wild rice.

meters) behind Spring Lake Dam. Within 30 years of its discovery, the plant had almost completely disappeared from Spring Lake. Its numbers were drastically reduced in other areas throughout its range. Today, Texas wild rice plants that flower are rarely seen.

The primary cause for the decline of this species has been the destruction of its habitat. The damming and dredging of the San Marcos River, an increase of sewage and chemical pollutants in the water, and human recreational activities, such as boating and swimming, have all played a role in damaging the plants' habitat.

Because of human population growth in the area, the flow of water from the San Marcos Springs has been reduced. Some experts predict that the flow will cease shortly after the year 2000. Efforts have been made to transplant Texas wild rice, but these efforts have been unsuccessful.

In order to save Texas wild rice, the U.S. Fish and Wildlife Service recommends that a public education program focusing on the plight of the plant be established. In addition, all remaining Texas wild rice habitat must be protected.

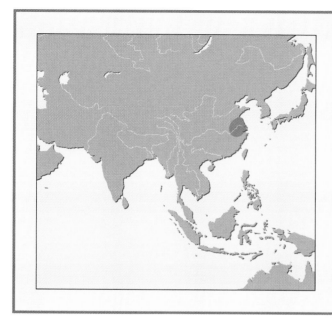

ALLIGATOR, CHINESE
Alligator sinensis

PHYLUM: Chordata
CLASS: Reptilia
ORDER: Crocodylia
FAMILY: Alligatoridae
STATUS: Critically endangered, IUCN
Endangered, ESA
RANGE: China

Alligator, Chinese
Alligator sinensis

Description and biology

There are only two species of alligator: the Chinese alligator and the American alligator. An average Chinese alligator measures 6 to 6.5 feet (1.8 to 2 meters) long, about 3 feet (0.9 meter) shorter than the American species. The Chinese alligator is dark olive in color with yellowish spots. It has a large head with a short, broad snout that turns up slightly. The alligator feeds on snails, freshwater mussels, fish, insects, and small mammals.

The Chinese alligator spends much of its life in burrows that it digs in the banks of rivers, streams, and ponds. It hibernates in a burrow from late October until early April. After emerging from hibernation, the alligator is active mainly during the day. In June, the beginning of the breeding season, the alligator becomes more nocturnal (active at night). After mating, a female Chinese alligator builds a mounded nest from dry leaves and grasses. She then lays 10 to 40 eggs

The Chinese alligator is only one of two species of alligator. The other is the American alligator.

between July and August. As the vegetation that makes up the nest begins to rot, the temperature inside the nest rises and the eggs begin to incubate (develop). When they hatch about 70 days later, the young alligators measure just over 8 inches (20 centimeters) long and weigh about 1 ounce (28 grams).

Habitat and current distribution

As its name indicates, the Chinese alligator is found in China. It is restricted to the lower valley of the Yangzi (Yangtze) River in Anhui (Anhwei), Zhejiang (Chekiang), and Jiangsu (Kiangsu) Provinces. Biologists (people who study living organisms) estimate that only about 130 Chinese alligators now exist in the wild. Most of these are found in Anhui Province. A large captive-breeding facility in Anhui holds another 10,000 alligators.

The Chinese alligator prefers to inhabit low beaches and dense stands of cane (type of plant) along the lower Yangzi River and its adjacent lakes and ponds.

History and conservation measures

The Chinese alligator once ranged more widely along the lower and middle Yangzi River Basin (region drained by the river and the streams that flow into it), as far west as Hunan and Hubei Provinces. As the human population in China has soared, the alligators' habitat has dwindled. Most contact between the alligators and humans has proven fatal for the alligators: they are often killed for food or because they are feared.

Environmental factors have also endangered the Chinese alligator. A flash flood can quickly trap an alligator, and if it cannot reach an air pocket or the water's surface, it drowns. A drought can reduce its habitat, forcing the alligator to search for water and suitable nesting sites. Because most remaining Chinese alligators inhabit wetlands and ponds that are scattered widely apart, drought remains a serious threat.

The Chinese government has given the Chinese alligator legal protection. In addition, several conservation areas have been set aside for the alligator, including the Wuhu Alligator Sanctuary in Anhui Province. Chongming Island, which is located near the mouth of the Yangtze River, is also being prepared for the establishment of a wild population of Chinese alligators.

ANOLE, CULEBRA ISLAND GIANT
Anolis roosevelti

PHYLUM: Chordata
CLASS: Reptilia
ORDER: Sauria
FAMILY: Iguanidae
STATUS: Critically endangered, IUCN
Endangered, ESA
RANGE: Puerto Rico

Anole, Culebra Island giant
Anolis roosevelti

Description and biology

The Culebra (pronounced koo–LAY–bra) Island giant anole (pronounced a–NO–lee), also known as Roosevelt's giant anole, is a large lizard that dwells in tree canopies (uppermost branchy layers of forests). The main part of its body is brown–gray. Its tail is yellow–brown and its belly is whitish. The anole's dewlap, or throat fan (loose skin hanging from its neck), is gray, bordered by light yellow. The adult male of the species has a scalloped fin that runs along its tail. An average adult measures about 6.5 inches (16.5 centimeters) long. The tail adds another 6 to 7 inches (15 to 18 centimeters).

Scientists know almost nothing about the Culebra Island giant anole's daily habits, reproduction, or life history. They believe it acts the same way as another species of anole in Puerto Rico. Based on observations of that species, scientists think that the giant anole is found mostly in tree canopies at heights between 49 and 82 feet (15 and 25 meters). It has a home range that may exceed 355 square feet (920 square meters). It probably has a varied diet consisting of many types of fruit and small animals.

The Culebra Island giant anole is a large lizard that dwells in the uppermost branchy layers of forests.

Habitat and current distribution

The Culebra Island giant anole once inhabited Culebra and Vieques Islands (part of Puerto Rico), Tortola Island (British Virgin Islands), and St. John Island (U.S. Virgin

Islands). All of these islands lie east of the Puerto Rican mainland.

Scientists are unable to estimate the total number of giant anoles currently in existence.

History and conservation measures

The Culebra Island giant anole is a rare and critically endangered species. The most recent specimens of the giant anole were collected on Culebra Island in 1932. Casual searches for the lizard on the northern section of the island in 1991 were unsuccessful.

Exactly why the giant anole is so rare, or if it is now extinct, is unknown. Although much of the forest area on Culebra Island has been cleared during the twentieth century, patches of canopy forest remained until Hurricane Hugo struck the island in 1989. Suitable forest habitat no longer remains on St. John. Canopy forest does remain on Tortola above 1,500 feet (457 meters) and probably also on Vieques. The clearing of forests by humans, introduced predators, and natural phenomena such as hurricanes have probably combined to reduce the number of giant anoles.

In 1982, the U.S. Fish and Wildlife Service approved a plan calling for the protection of remaining giant anole habitat on Culebra Island. The plan also called for systematic searches of the island to locate any remaining giant anoles. So far, those intense searches have not been undertaken. Scientists are hopeful that the Culebra Island giant anole survives on at least one of the islands in its original range.

BOA, PUERTO RICAN
Epicrates inornatus

PHYLUM: Chordata
CLASS: Reptilia
ORDER: Serpentes
FAMILY: Boidae
STATUS: Lower risk, near threatened, IUCN Endangered, ESA
RANGE: Puerto Rico

Boa, Puerto Rican
Epicrates inornatus

Description and biology

The Puerto Rican boa is usually dark or mahogany brown in color. The dorsal section or back of this snake has a series of narrow angular blotches with dark brown or black edges. Many larger, older Puerto Rican boas have virtually no patterns. The venter, or belly, is dark brown to gray in color with dark brown marks. The inside of the snake's mouth is black. Most adult Puerto Rican boas measure 5 to 6.5 feet (1.5 to 2 meters) long and weigh 4.4 to 6.6 pounds (2 to 3 kilograms). Large boas may reach a length of over 8 feet (2.4 meters).

The Puerto Rican boa is nocturnal (active at night). It may be found both on the ground and in trees. It hunts a variety of small prey, including bats, rodents, and small birds. The

The Puerto Rican boa is nocturnal (active at night). It hunts a variety of small prey, including bats, rodents, and small birds.

boa captures its prey by biting it and wrapping its body around it at the same time. The prey eventually suffocates because it is unable to expand its rib cage. The boa then swallows the prey whole, as other snakes do.

Mating takes place between April and May. Although a male Puerto Rican boa will attempt to mate with a female every year, she will give birth only every other year, usually to 10 to 32 young between August and October.

Habitat and current distribution

This snake is widespread in Puerto Rico, except in the arid (dry) southwest portion of the island. It is most abundant in the Caribbean National Forest. Although the boa prefers to inhabit rain forests and plantations, it has also been found in subtropical dry forests and even urban areas.

History and conservation measures

The Puerto Rican boa was placed on the Endangered Species List in 1970, making it one of the first species protected by the U.S. Endangered Species Act. The boa's population initially declined because large tracts of forest on Puerto Rico were cleared to create farmland. Recently, however, many people living in rural areas have moved to the island's cities, and their farms have grown into forests once again. Because of this, the boa made a dramatic recovery during the 1990s, but has remained in endangered status.

The boa receives further protection on the island under the Regulation to Govern the Management of Threatened and Endangered Species in the Commonwealth of Puerto Rico. Despite this legal proclamation, the boa is still threatened by some rural Puerto Ricans, who believe the fat of the Puerto Rican boa can be used as a medicine. As a result, they kill the snake to extract its fat.

CAIMAN, BLACK
Melanosuchus niger

PHYLUM: Chordata
CLASS: Reptilia
ORDER: Crocodylia
FAMILY: Alligatoridae
STATUS: Lower risk, conservation dependent, IUCN Endangered, ESA
RANGE: Bolivia, Brazil, Colombia, Ecuador, French Guiana, Guyana, Paraguay, Peru, Venezuela

Caiman, black

Melanosuchus niger

Description and biology

The black caiman is the largest species of crocodile in the Western Hemisphere. While an average adult measures 13 to 15 feet (4 to 4.6 meters) long, some black caimans have been known to exceed 20 feet (6 meters). A mature black caiman is black with lighter brown blotches on its head. A young caiman has spots of yellow, green, or white on its head, and its underside is pale. The crocodile eats a variety of small animals (especially rodents) and fish (particularly catfish and piranha). It also preys on small deer, cattle, and other caiman.

Many aspects of the black caiman's reproductive habits are unknown. What is known is that the breeding season varies from September to January, depending on geographic location. Hatching takes place from November to March. A

678

female black caiman builds a mound nest out of leaves, twigs, and other plant debris. This mound often measures 5 feet (1.5 meters) wide and 2.6 feet (0.8 meter) high. The female then lays a clutch of 30 to 60 hard–shelled eggs into the nest and covers them. As the plant matter decays, the temperature inside the nest rises, causing the eggs to incubate (develop). They hatch after 5 to 6 weeks.

The head of a young black caiman showing its colorful spots. After maturing, the caiman's spots change to light–brown blotches.

Habitat and current distribution

The black caiman is found throughout the Amazon Basin (area drained by the Amazon River). The largest known concentration of caimans—as many as 1,000—used to be in French Guiana, but uncontrolled hunting has reduced that population. Biologists (people who study living organisms) are unsure of the total number of existing black caimans.

Black caimans prefer to inhabit freshwater ecosystems (living things and their environment). In particular, they seek out undisturbed backwaters, or bends in lagoons and large rivers. They are also found in flooded forest and grassland areas.

History and conservation measures

The black caiman once existed in great numbers throughout the entire Amazonian region. Hunting for its hide has been the major reason for its decline. The crocodile's large size made it an easy target for hunters, who killed millions of black caimans for the leather industry. Serious hunting began in the 1940s and continued until the early 1970s, when the demand for alligator leather decreased and hunters could no longer make a profit. However, poaching (illegal hunting) of the crocodile continues in some areas.

The black caiman is also threatened by habitat loss. Large areas in its range have been cleared by loggers or converted into farms or cattle ranches. Considering the caiman a threat to livestock, many ranchers have killed the animal.

The decline of the black caiman has had a dramatic impact on the region's ecology. One of the animals the caiman preys on is the capybara, the largest member of the rodent family. As the caiman population has decreased, the capybara population has increased. These rodents have caused considerable damage to crops in certain areas of Bolivia and Brazil. The piranha population has also increased because of a decline in the number of caiman. As a result, many cattle have been attacked and killed as they have tried to cross flooded grasslands.

Even a decline in the amount of black caiman excrement (waste matter) has thrown the region's ecology out of balance. This excrement is an important part of the food chain, particularly for zooplankton (microscopic aquatic animals) and phytoplankton (microscopic aquatic plants). Each is an important part of the diet of fish hatchlings. Consequently, the decreasing number of black caiman has resulted in a decreasing number of some fish species.

The black caiman is legally protected in most of the countries in which it is found, but the laws are poorly enforced. Important protected areas for the caiman include the Manu National Park in Peru and the Parque Nacional de Amazonia in Brazil. A program to breed black caimans in captivity and then release them into the wild was established in Bolivia. Some of these programs have clearly paid off. In several different areas the black caiman population increased significantly during the 1990s. In 1999, the International Union for the Conservation of Nature and Natural Resources (IUCN) concluded that the species was no longer threatened with extinction and upgraded its status from endangered to lower risk.

Crocodile, American

Crocodylus acutus

Description and biology

The American crocodile grows to an average length of 12 feet (3.6 meters), but is capable of reaching lengths between 15 and 20 feet (4.5 and 6 meters). It has a slender snout and a hump on its forehead between its eyes. Mature American crocodiles are dark brown to dark greenish–brown in color. Young or juvenile crocodiles are light greenish–brown with dark markings on their bodies and tails. Their undersides, or bellies, are pale. This species of crocodile feeds primarily on fish, but also eats birds, crabs, small mammals, snakes, and turtles.

Once having mated, a female American crocodile will build a nest and lay about 40 eggs around the beginning of May. The nest can be either a hole dug in the sand on a beach

or a mound built out of plant debris (leaves and other matter). These mounds vary in size: they can reach up to 15 feet (4.5 meters) in diameter and 2 feet (0.6 meter) in height. The female may use this same nest year after year. Once they hatch around the beginning of August, young crocodiles face a tough challenge. They are often preyed on by birds, crabs, raccoons, and even adult crocodiles. Very few survive to full adulthood.

Crocodile hides are valuable because they are used to make items such as shoes, belts, and handbags. As a result, crocodiles have been overhunted and their numbers have declined greatly.

Habitat and current distribution

The American crocodile is found in southern Florida, the southern coasts of Mexico, Central America, northern South America, and on the Caribbean islands of Cuba, Jamaica, and Hispaniola (divided between the Dominican Republic on the east and Haiti on the west). Biologists (people who study living organisms) estimate that about 200 to 400 crocodiles exist in the Florida Keys, but they are unsure of the total world population size.

American crocodiles prefer to inhabit coastal waters, including brackish areas (where freshwater and salt water mix) of rivers and lagoons. A number of crocodiles inhabit inland freshwater areas.

History and conservation measures

At one time, the American crocodile was abundant. But its numbers have been greatly reduced by the hunt for its valuable hide. The crocodile is protected in 8 of the 17 countries in which it exists, but this protection is not enforced. Illegal hunting continues in some areas. In recent decades, the development of cities and farms in the crocodile's range have robbed it of much of its habitat, causing a further drop in its numbers.

The hide of the American crocodile is still quite valuable. Crocodile ranches or farms have been established in five countries to breed crocodiles specifically to meet the demand for their hides. Conservationists (people who protect the natural world) urge officials to monitor these farms to see that no wild American crocodiles are captured to build up captive populations.

CROCODILE, ORINOCO
Crocodylus intermedius

PHYLUM: Chordata
CLASS: Reptilia
ORDER: Crocodylia
FAMILY: Crocodylidae
STATUS: Critically endangered, IUCN
Endangered, ESA
RANGE: Colombia, Venezuela

Crocodile, Orinoco

Crocodylus intermedius

Description and biology

The Orinoco (pronounced or–i–NO–coe) crocodile is a very large crocodile that grows to an average length between 11 and 17 feet (3.4 and 5.2 meters). Some exceptionally large males of the species have been observed as being 23 feet (7 meters) long. The upper body of the crocodile is dark green to tan in color with dark markings. Its underside is lighter. It has a long nose and a narrow, slightly upturned snout. It feeds primarily on fish, small mammals, and birds.

After mating, a female Orinoco crocodile digs a hole in an exposed sandbar in a river in January or February (the dry season) and lays 40 to 70 eggs. The eggs hatch about 70 days later, when the river begins to rise during the wet season. The female protects her young for 1 to 3 years.

Even with protected habitats in which to live, Orinoco crocodiles are still in danger of becoming extinct due to illegal hunting.

Habitat and current distribution

This crocodile species is found only in the Orinoco River Basin (area drained by the Orinoco River) in eastern Colombia and Venezuela. It is considered almost extinct in Colombia and very rare in Venezuela. Biologists (people who study living organisms) believe fewer than 1,500 Orinoco crocodiles currently survive in the wild.

The Orinoco crocodile prefers to inhabit wide and very deep parts of large rivers. During the wet season, when river currents are strong, the crocodile occupies lakes and pools.

History and conservation measures

Up until the 1930s, the Orinoco crocodile was considered to be very common. Now it is one of the most critically endangered crocodiles in the Western Hemisphere. Its large, high–quality hide is valuable to hunters. From 1930 through the 1950s, hunters nearly wiped out the Orinoco crocodile population. The species has never recovered from the on-slaught.

Hunting remains a threat to the Orinoco crocodile. Humans in the region kill the crocodile for a number of reasons, including using its eggs and meat for food and its teeth for medicines. The crocodile now faces the added threat of habitat loss as human populations expand into its range.

In Venezuela, a newly created national park, Parque Nacional Santos Luzardo, provides protected habitat for the Orinoco crocodile. A recently declared wildlife refuge has also been established along the Guaritico River in western Venezuela. This area was the site of the first release of captive–bred crocodiles into the wild. Despite these protected areas, the Orinoco crocodile faces continued threats in Venezuela and Colombia as laws protecting it are not well enforced in either country.

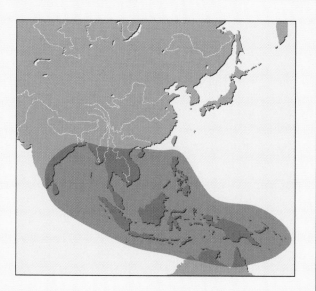

Crocodile, saltwater

Crocodylus porosus

Description and biology

The saltwater crocodile, also known as the estuarine crocodile or Indopacific crocodile, is one of the largest living crocodiles on Earth. It measures between 10 and 23 feet (3 and 7 meters) in length and weighs over 2,000 pounds (908 kilograms). It has a large head, a long snout, and webbed hind feet. The upper part of a mature saltwater crocodile's body is dark green to black in color. Its belly is yellow or cream. This crocodile's diet includes fish, snakes, birds, turtles, cattle, horses, and even humans. The saltwater crocodile sometimes drags its prey under the water to eat later.

Male saltwater crocodiles reach sexual maturity around 16 years of age; females reach sexual maturity at 10 years. The breeding season varies with geographic location, but most often occurs during an area's wet season. After building a mound nest out of leaves, grass, reeds, mud, and other plant debris, a female lays 40 to 60 eggs inside the mound. As the plant mat-

ter making up the nest begins to decompose, the temperature inside the nest rises and the eggs begin to incubate (develop). After 80 to 90 days, the eggs hatch. Sharks and other aquatic predators often prey on the young saltwater crocodiles.

Although it is considered endangered, the saltwater crocodile is one of the most abundant crocodile species left on Earth.

Habitat and current distribution

The saltwater crocodile is the most widespread crocodile species. It is found in Southeast Asia, Indonesia, the Philippines, New Guinea, and northern Australia. It is at risk throughout most of its range, except in Australia (where it is at low risk of extinction). Biologists (people who study living organisms) estimate that tens of thousands of saltwater crocodiles currently exist.

The saltwater crocodile prefers to inhabit coastal brackish waters and the tidal sections of rivers—areas where freshwater and salt water mix. However, it has also been found in fresh-water rivers and inland swamps and marshes.

History and conservation measures

Like many other crocodile species, the saltwater crocodile has diminished in number mainly because of hunting for its hide. The loss of its habitat has also contributed to its decline.

Hunters like the hide of this crocodile because it produces a large quantity of valued leather. During the 1950s and 1960s, hundreds of thousands of saltwater crocodiles were killed every year to satisfy the demand for crocodile leather. International treaties now regulate the trade of this species. Since the crocodile's range extends over such a large area, however, illegal hunting and trade are difficult to control.

Habitat loss further threatens the remaining saltwater crocodiles. Coastal mangrove habitats, in particular, have been steadily cleared and drained to create farmland throughout the crocodile's range.

In Papua New Guinea, a controversial program has been established whereby newly hatched saltwater crocodiles are taken from the wild and reared in captivity. After three years, they are killed for their hides. Supporters of this program say many of these young crocodiles would have been killed by predators in the wild. Using their hides satisfies the commercial demand for leather without damaging the species in the wild. Opponents believe the program hurts the saltwater crocodile population because many of the young crocodiles are not even given the chance to survive in the wild.

In the Bhitarkanika National Park in India, a captive-breeding program has been quite successful. A number of the saltwater crocodiles that were raised in captivity and then released into the wild have begun to breed.

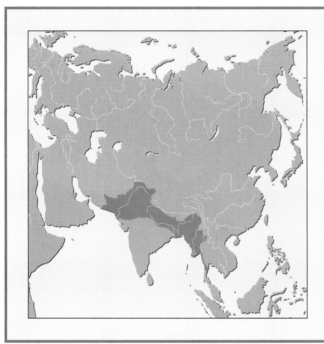

GAVIAL
Gavialis gangeticus

PHYLUM: Chordata
CLASS: Reptilia
ORDER: Crocodylia
FAMILY: Gavialidae
STATUS: Endangered, IUCN Endangered, ESA
RANGE: Bangladesh, Bhutan, India, Nepal, Pakistan

Gavial

Gavialis gangeticus

Description and biology

The gavial (pronounced GAY–vee–al), also known as the gharial (pronounced GER–ee–al), is a large member of the crocodile order. It has an average body and tail length of 13 to 20 feet (4 to 6 meters). The gavial has a long, slender snout with parallel sides and narrow, sharp teeth—quite different from alligators and crocodiles. In fact, the gavial's teeth are the sharpest of any member of the crocodile order. The gavial is olive green to brown–gray in color on its upper body and lighter underneath. It feeds primarily on small fish and only occasionally on birds, dogs, and goats. It rarely eats humans.

Mature males of the species have a growth of tissue next to their nostrils. The tissue is shaped like an earthen pot, known as a "ghara" in north India. Many believe this is how the animal received its common name.

691

A member of the crocodile family, the Indian gavial, or gharial, has the sharpest teeth of all crocodiles.

Around the beginning of April, after having mated, the female gavial digs a hole in a sandbank and lays a clutch (eggs produced at one time) of 30 to 50 oval–shaped eggs. The eggs hatch after 83 to 94 days. Since predators threaten the eggs and the young gavials, the female gavial guards the nest and protects the young for a period of several months after they are born.

Habitat and current distribution

The gavial is almost extinct in Bangladesh, Bhutan, and Pakistan. It is critically endangered in India and Nepal. Biologists (people who study living organisms) believe fewer than 150 gavials exist in the wild.

The gavial prefers to inhabit high–banked rivers with clear, fast–flowing water and deep pools.

History and conservation measures

The gavial was still quite common in many areas in its range at the beginning of the twentieth century. Since then, its population has been severely reduced by the loss of its habitat and hunting for its hide.

The fast–flowing rivers favored by gavials are prime sites for the building of dams and reservoirs, which are used for hydroelectric facilities or for irrigation projects. When a dam or reservoir is constructed, the gavial's habitat is destroyed as sandbanks and deep pools both upstream and downstream of the site are eliminated.

Hunting of the gavial, once widespread, has declined since countries in the animal's range have passed laws protecting it. Large–scale commercial hunting no longer takes place, but illegal hunting by individual hunters still occurs.

Programs to aid in the recovery of the gavial have been established. In one program, gavial eggs are collected in the wild and then hatched in captivity. The captive–bred young are then released into protected areas in the wild. Although this program has been successful, the species' numbers remain dangerously low. Gavials inhabit several protected areas in India, the Royal Chitwan National Park in Nepal, and a reserve in Pakistan.

GECKO, MONITO
Sphaerodactylus micropithecus

PHYLUM: Chordata
CLASS: Reptilia
ORDER: Sauria
FAMILY: Gekkonidae
STATUS: Endangered, IUCN
Endangered, ESA
RANGE: Commonwealth of
Puerto Rico

Gecko, Monito

Sphaerodactylus micropithecus

Description and biology

The Monito gecko is a tiny lizard that grows to be about 1.5 inches (4 centimeters) long from tail to snout. It has a flattened body covered in mottled dark brown or gray scales. Its tail is tan. The Monito gecko has short limbs, each equipped with tiny suction cups for climbing around on cliffs. Its bulging eyes are protected by transparent scales. Monito geckos are quite vocal—they croak, bark, squeak, and make clicking noises.

Monito geckos are nocturnal (active at night). They eat an assortment of insects, including beetles, flies, crickets, spiders, and ants. Eating is generally done in groups. No studies have been done on their life cycles, so information is limited. Scientists do know that their mating season is from March to November. A Monito gecko in the wild probably lives from four to ten years.

694

Habitat and current distribution

Monito geckos can be found only in the Commonwealth of Puerto Rico on Monito Island, a small island located 3 miles (5 kilometers) northwest of Mona Island in the Mona Passage midway between Puerto Rico and the Dominican Republic. A thorough two–day survey of Monito Island in 1982 turned up about 18 of these geckos. Although wildlife biologists (people who study living organisms) do not know the population of the Monito gecko, it is probably somewhat higher than the 18 that were found in the survey.

Monito Island is surrounded on all sides by 100– to 150–foot cliffs. The top of the island is flat and composed of limestone (a form of rock) covered in cacti, shrubs, and stunted trees that manage to grow through cracks in the limestone. When the island was surveyed for Monito geckos in

Monito geckos can be found only on the small island of Monito in the Commonwealth of Puerto Rico.

1982, they were found only in two small areas. The places where they were found, though, did not seem to differ from other parts of the island.

History and conservation measures

Although geckos of a different species on nearby Mona Island are abundant and well known, the Monito gecko was not discovered until 1974. At that time, scientists found one adult male and one egg on Monito Island. They hatched the egg in a laboratory and then released the animals on the island. Until 1982, no Monito geckos were found, even when the island was surveyed. Then 18 were found in 1982. By all indications, this has long been a very rare animal.

Black rats, introduced to Monito Island decades ago, have probably been responsible for the very low population of the species. Because the population is so dangerously low, the entire area of Monito Island has been designated as critical habitat (area necessary for the protection and preservation of a species that has been listed under the Endangered Species Act. Critical habitat designation does not create a wildlife refuge or eliminate human activities in the area.)

The U.S. Fish and Wildlife Service recommends a complete biological study of the Monito gecko for future recovery plans.

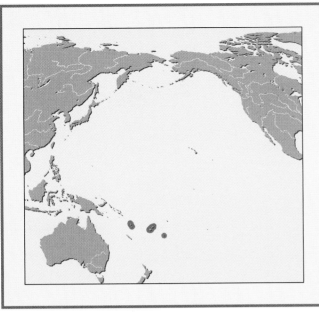

IGUANA, FIJI BANDED
Brachylophus fasciatus

PHYLUM: Chordata
CLASS: Reptilia
ORDER: Sauria
FAMILY: Iguanidae
STATUS: Endangered, IUCN Endangered, ESA
RANGE: Fiji, Tonga, Vanuatu

Iguana, Fiji banded

Brachylophus fasciatus

Description and biology

The Fiji banded iguana is so–named because males of the species have pale, bluish–green bands covering their green bodies. Females are usually entirely green. The banded iguana's skin color changes in response to light, temperature, and its mood. The male's banding is most obvious when courting a female or when fighting with another male.

Adult Fiji banded iguanas have a body length of about 7.5 inches (19 centimeters). Their tails measure two to three times their body length. Males are generally longer than females. This species has salt glands in the nasal area, and salt is expelled when the iguana sneezes. Biologists (people who study living organisms), however, do not fully understand the purpose of these glands. These banded iguanas are primarily vegetarians, feeding on leaves, fruit, and flowers. They occasionally eat insects.

Male Fiji banded iguanas are territorial and aggressive. They fight among themselves to determine who is dominant.

Although females of the species are entirely green, male Fiji banded iguanas have bluish–green bands covering their bodies.

Once determined, only the dominant male mates with available females. A male's courtship behavior includes head bobbing and a display of his banding and bright coloration. After mating with a dominant male, a female Fiji banded iguana digs a burrow, or hole, into which she lays three or four eggs. She then covers the burrow with dirt and the eggs are left to incubate (develop).

Habitat and current distribution

The Fiji banded iguana exists on various islands that are a part of the island nations of Fiji, Tonga, and Vanuatu (New Hebrides) in the southwest Pacific Ocean. On Kandavu, one of the Fiji Islands, the banded iguana is considered to be abundant, but it is seldom seen. Biologists are unsure of the total number of Fiji banded iguanas currently in existence.

This iguana prefers to inhabit dense, undisturbed forests.

History and conservation measures

The clearing of its forest habitat is the main reason the Fiji banded iguana has declined or disappeared from many islands in its range. Biologists have found it difficult to monitor or study the banded iguana in the wild: the animal is hard to find because it is secretive by nature and its coloring provides excellent camouflaging.

The banded iguana breeds well in captivity, and several zoos currently have breeding programs. If this animal becomes critically endangered in the near future, then captive–bred Fiji banded iguanas may be reintroduced into the wild.

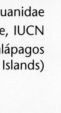

IGUANA, GALÁPAGOS LAND
Conolophus subcristatus

PHYLUM: Chordata
CLASS: Reptilia
ORDER: Sauria
FAMILY: Iguanidae
STATUS: Vulnerable, IUCN
RANGE: Ecuador (Galápagos Islands)

Iguana, Galápagos land
Conolophus subcristatus

Description and biology

The Galápagos land iguana is a large iguana with a stout body. It has well–developed limbs, a moderately long tail, a large head with prominent jaw muscles, and a spiny crest running along its back. The largest land iguanas reach a length of almost 4 feet (1.2 meters). Males, which are always at least twice as heavy as females, weigh an average of about 15.4 pounds (7 kilograms). This iguana is yellowish–brown in color with patches of black, brown, and rust.

Like other large iguanas, the Galápagos land iguana is primarily a vegetarian. It eats low–ground plants and shrubs, as well as the fallen fruit and pads, or leaves, of cactus trees. These succulent pads provide the iguana with most of the moisture it needs during dry periods. During the midday heat, iguanas seek out the shade provided by cactus trees or other

vegetation. At night, to conserve heat, they sleep in burrows they have dug in the ground.

Male land iguanas are very territorial and often aggressive toward one another. They patrol the boundaries of their territories and deter intruders with various displays, including rapid head nodding. More than one female usually inhabits the territory of a single male. In July, a few weeks after mating, a female land iguana lays 7 to 25 eggs in a burrow she has dug 1.6 feet (0.5 meter) deep in soft sand or volcanic ash. The young iguanas hatch about 14 weeks later, taking almost a week to dig their way out of the nest.

Habitat and current distribution

The Galápagos land iguana is found only on the Galápagos Islands of Fernandina, Isabela, Santa Cruz, Santa Fe,

Predators such as cats, dogs, and pigs are the reason for the decline of the Galápagos land iguana population.

Seymour, and South Plaza (the Galápagos Islands are a province of Ecuador, lying about 600 miles [965 kilometers] off the west coast of the country). Biologists (people who study living organisms) sometimes regard the population on Sante Fe Island as a second species of Galápagos land iguana (*Conolophus pallidus*). The *Conolophus pallidus* is given endangered status on the U.S. Fish and Wildlife Service's endangered species list.

Land iguanas prefer dry areas on the islands they inhabit.

History and conservation measures

Whalers and settlers began visiting the Galápagos Islands at the beginning of the nineteenth century. At that time, the Galápagos land iguana was quite abundant. When English naturalist Charles Darwin (1809–1882) visited the Galápagos island of Santiago in 1835, he found the island covered with their burrows. Today, the Santiago Island land iguanas Darwin wrote about have disappeared.

Galápagos land iguanas did not fall prey to the settlers or even native predators (snakes and hawks). Instead, they were decimated by introduced predators, such as the cats, pigs, dogs, goats, and other domestic animals the settlers brought to the islands. Over time, many of these animals escaped or were abandoned. They became wild and their populations grew on the islands. Wild pigs dug up iguana nests to feed on the eggs. Wild cats killed young iguanas, while wild dogs killed adults. Wild goats fed on the iguana's food source.

In 1959, the Ecuadoran government declared all uninhabited areas in the Galápagos a national park. This declaration meant that land iguanas and other island species could not be hunted, captured, or disturbed. In the mid–1970s, a captive–breeding program for the iguanas was established on Santa Cruz island. More than 250 Galápagos land iguanas have been raised in captivity and then returned to the wild. Programs to rid the Galápagos Islands of introduced animals are in progress.

LIZARD, BLUNT–NOSED LEOPARD
Gambelia silus (or sila)

PHYLUM: Chordata
CLASS: Reptilia
ORDER: Sauria
FAMILY: Iguanidae
STATUS: Endangered, IUCN
Endangered, ESA
RANGE: USA (California)

Lizard, blunt-nosed leopard
Gambelia silus (or sila)

Description and biology

As its name indicates, this lizard has a blunt nose and a leopard–like pattern on its body. To help regulate the lizard's body temperature, its color and pattern change throughout the day: in the morning, when it is cool, dark spots and light sand–colored bars appear on the surface of the lizard's body; as the temperature rises during the day, the pattern fades to a lighter shade.

This lizard species also changes color during mating season. During courtship, the sides of males turn salmon or light pink. After having mated, females develop rusty–orange to red blotches on their sides that remain until they lay their eggs.

An average blunt–nosed leopard lizard has a body length of 3.5 to 5 inches (8.9 to 12.7 centimeters). Its tail can often reach a length of 8 inches (20 centimeters). If a predator such

The blunt–nosed leopard lizard's color and pattern change throughout the day to help regulate its body temperature.

as a squirrel, skunk, shrike (type of bird), or snake catches the lizard by its tail, the lizard can shed the tail and grow a new one. The blunt–nosed leopard lizard feeds on grasshoppers, caterpillars, flies, bees, and occasionally other young lizards. This species may also eat its own young.

The blunt–nosed leopard lizard spends its winter hibernating in a deep burrow made by a rodent or other small animal. It emerges from hibernation around the beginning of April, and is then active only during the coolest hours of the day. Mating season takes place during May and June. A single male may defend a territory that includes several females. After mating, a female enters a burrow in June or July to lay a clutch of two or three eggs. The eggs hatch in August.

Habitat and current distribution

Sometimes called the San Joaquin leopard lizard, this lizard species is found only in parts of the San Joaquin Valley and adjacent foothills in south–central California. Biologists (people who study living organisms) do not know the total number of blunt–nosed leopard lizards in existence.

The lizard species inhabits grassland, scrub (stunted trees and shrubs), and plains areas. It cannot survive in cultivated areas (farmland and urban areas).

History and conservation measures

The blunt–nosed leopard lizard once ranged throughout the San Joaquin Valley. For the most part, this species has diminished in number because much of its habitat has been converted into farmland and urban areas. By the 1950s, 50 percent of the lizard's original habitat had been lost. By the early 1980s, only about 100,000 acres (40,000 hectares) of suitable habitat remained.

Since the lizard cannot survive in cultivated areas, the only way to save it is to protect its remaining habitat. Conservationists are in the process of obtaining land throughout the blunt–nosed leopard lizard's range to set aside as reserves for the animal.

LIZARD, HIERRO GIANT
Gallotia simonyi

PHYLUM: Chordata
CLASS: Reptilia
ORDER: Sauria
FAMILY: Lacertidae
STATUS: Critically endangered, IUCN
Endangered, ESA
RANGE: Spain

Lizard, Hierro giant
Gallotia simonyi

Description and biology

The Hierro (pronounced YER–o) giant lizard is large compared to other lizards in its family (called lacertids). This lizard can have a body length up to 7.5 inches (19 centimeters) and a total length (including its tail) over 20 inches (51 centimeters). Most other lacertids are about one–third this size. The body of the Hierro giant lizard is greenish–brown in color with a few large, pale yellow–tinged spots on the sides. The lizard's head is yellowish–brown on top with irregular black marks. Around and under its jaw are large scales dotted by large pale spots surrounded by black.

Hierro giant lizards eat mainly plants, but will feed on insects such as bumblebees, grasshoppers, and ants. Once morning sunlight strikes the cliff on which they live, the lizards emerge from hiding in rock crevices. They are active all day, except for a short period around midday.

Biologists (people who study living organisms) do not have much information regarding the Hierro giant lizard's reproductive habits. They believe that a female, after having mated, lays a clutch (eggs produced at one time) of up to eight eggs in September in a small pocket in the sand. Some biologists think that females may lay their eggs as early as April and may breed only every other year.

Habitat and current distribution

The entire Hierro giant lizard population—totaling about 100 lizards—lives in a small area halfway up a steep cliff face on Hierro, the westernmost island in the Canary Islands (a province of Spain, this island group lies off the northwest coast of Africa, along the border between Western Sahara and Morocco).

The cliff the lizards inhabit is known on the island as Fuga de Gorreta. Hierro is volcanic in origin and very rocky, and this cliff has many boulders and crevices that provide the Hierro giant lizards with shelter. The lizards are found in an area between 1,150 and 1,640 feet (350 and 500 meters) in altitude.

History and conservation measures

Scientists first began collecting specimens of the Hierro giant lizard in the late nineteenth century. At the time, the lizard was found over most of Hierro. By the late 1930s, however, the lizard had disappeared from many areas largely due to over–collection or capture. Since then, human development of the island and introduced predators (mainly cats and dogs) have reduced the Hierro giant lizard population to a single group on Fuga de Gorreta.

ICONA, a Spanish conservation agency, has designed a recovery plan for the Hierro giant lizard that includes protecting its remaining habitat and establishing a captive–breeding program. Although the plan has recently been set in motion, it is still too early to gauge the results.

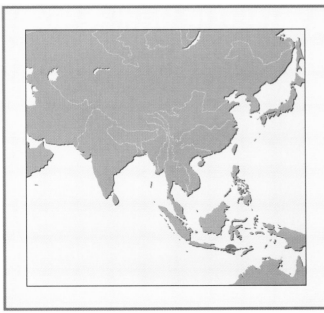

MONITOR, KOMODO ISLAND
Varanus komodoensis

PHYLUM: Chordata
CLASS: Reptilia
ORDER: Sauria
FAMILY: Varanidae
STATUS: Vulnerable, IUCN
Endangered, ESA
RANGE: Indonesia

Monitor, Komodo Island

Varanus komodoensis

Description and biology

The Komodo Island monitor, also called the Komodo dragon or "ora" by the people of Komodo, is the largest living lizard on Earth. An average adult can measure up to 10 feet (3 meters) long and weigh 300 pounds (136 kilograms). Despite its size, it can move quickly on the ground and is an agile swimmer and climber. The monitor has a dark gray, stocky body and stout, powerful legs with sharply clawed feet. It has a large head and a long, forked tongue that it uses to "taste" the air, following the scent of its prey.

The monitor feeds on wild pigs, deer, water buffalo, dogs, goats, rats, snakes, birds, other monitors, and, if given the chance, humans. It attacks by ambushing its prey, lunging from the tall grass of its savanna habitat. The monitor has razor–sharp serrated teeth. One bite is often enough to subdue its prey. If the prey happens to escape, it usually will not live long. The mouth of a monitor is filled with poisonous

Despite being the largest living lizard on Earth, the Komodo Island monitor, also known as the Komodo dragon, can move quickly on the ground and is a good swimmer and climber.

bacteria. The bite area becomes infected over the course of a few days, and the prey weakens to the point when it can no longer flee. The monitor then moves in and devours the prey completely—nothing is left. The monitor's yellow tongue and foul mouth odor (caused by the bacteria present) may have inspired legends of fire–breathing dragons.

After mating, female Komodo Island monitors lay 15 to 30 eggs with smooth, leatherlike shells in a hole. They usually lay eggs several times between July and early September. The eggs hatch after about 34 weeks. For the first year of their lives, young monitors live in trees and feed on insects. When they have grown to a length of about 3 feet (0.9 meter), they move to the ground. This helps protect them from predators, including adult monitors.

Habitat and current distribution

The Komodo Island monitor is found only on Komodo, Rintja, and western Flores Islands in Indonesia. Biologists (people who study living organisms) estimate the monitor's total population to be between 4,000 and 5,000.

Monitors prefer to inhabit dry savanna, woodland thickets, and forest fringes and clearings.

History and conservation measures

The Komodo Island monitor once occupied many Indonesian islands. It was discovered on Komodo Island in 1912. Since that time, its population has been drastically reduced—mainly by humans. The monitor has been hunted for sport, for collections, and for its hide. Although laws now limit commercial hunting, the monitor is still sometimes poisoned by villagers who believe it is a threat to children and domestic animals.

The over–hunting of deer by humans in the monitor's range has reduced its available prey. Its habitat also has been reduced by the burning and clearing of woodland to create farmland and villages. The monitor is further disturbed by hordes of tourists who travel to Komodo Island specifically to see the world's largest lizard. The Indonesian government is currently trying to regulate this "ecotourism."

A capitive–breeding program has not been successful in saving the Komodo Island monitors since they do not reproduce well in captivity. They often die from diseases and infections.

PYTHON, INDIAN
Python molurus

PHYLUM: Chordata
CLASS: Reptilia
ORDER: Serpentes
FAMILY: Boidae
STATUS: Lower risk: near threatened, IUCN Endangered, ESA
RANGE: Bangladesh, Cambodia, China, India, Indonesia, Laos, Myanmar, Nepal, Pakistan, Sri Lanka, Thailand, Vietnam

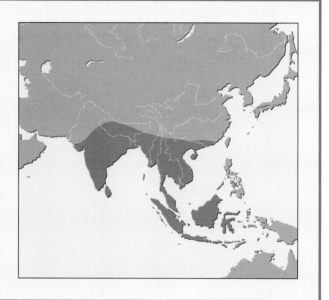

Python, Indian

Python molurus

Description and biology

The Indian python is large and heavy–bodied. One of the world's largest snakes, it averages 10 feet (3 meters) long, but has been known to grow to lengths over 20 feet (6 meters). This snake is straw–yellow to brown in color, sometimes with a rich reddish tinge. The dark patterns that form a mosaic on the snake's skin differ depending on the snake's geographic location.

Indian pythons prey on birds and other reptiles, but prefer small mammals such as rats. It is not unusual for a python, which is a good climber, to climb a fruit tree and then wait in ambush for animals attracted to the fallen fruit underneath. Pythons have also been observed waiting in hollow trees to capture roosting birds.

In India, mating between male and female Indian pythons takes place from December to February. After mating, a female may lay between 6 and 100 eggs at one time. An average clutch

size is 35 eggs. The eggs are laid in a rock crevice, termite nest, tree hole, or other convenient shelter. The female remains with the eggs throughout the 100–day incubation (development) period (she leaves them only to drink water). She warms the eggs by wrapping her body around them. Biologists (people who study living organisms) believe the female controls her body temperature by constricting, or twitching, her muscles, which would regulate the amount of blood flowing to the surface of her body. Upon hatching, the young pythons average around 21 inches (53 centimeters) in length.

A coiled Indian python. Female pythons coil their bodies around their eggs in order to warm them and aid them in hatching.

Habitat and current distribution

The Indian python is widespread in Asia. It ranges from Pakistan in the west to China in the east. It is found as far south as parts of Indonesia. Biologists usually divide the species into two subspecies: a western form in the South Asian subcontinent (*Python molurus molurus*) and an eastern form in China and Southeast Asia (*Python molurus bivittatus*). Of the two subspecies, the western subspecies is the more endangered. Biologists have no estimate of the total number of Indian pythons in existence.

Indian pythons are found in a variety of habitats, but prefer wooded areas, ranging from evergreen rain forest to open dry scrubland.

History and conservation measures

The Indian python is still found in most parts of its historic range, but its numbers have declined. The main reason has been habitat loss, and this remains a major threat to the python. Human populations in the snake's range have soared. In India alone, the population has more than tripled in the twentieth century. Advances in modern farming technology have allowed humans to convert "waste lands" such as scrubland into farmland.

Indian pythons have also been hunted for their skin to make belts, boots, wallets, and other fashion accessories. International treaties now regulate the trade of python skins. Nonetheless, people in some Asian cultures still hunt the snake for food and for use as a medicine.

Like other snakes, the Indian python is regarded simply as dangerous and is often killed on sight. Many people, however, do not realize the ecological role the python plays. As the Indian python population has decreased in many areas, the rodent population has correspondingly increased.

SNAKE, SAN FRANCISCO GARTER
Thamnophis sirtalis tetrataenia

PHYLUM: Chordata
CLASS: Reptilia
ORDER: Serpentes
FAMILY: Colubridae
STATUS: Endangered, ESA
RANGE: USA (California)

Snake, San Francisco garter

Thamnophis sirtalis tetrataenia

Description and biology

For those who love snakes, the San Francisco garter snake is thought to be one of the most beautiful varieties. Adult San Francisco garter snakes grow to be about 51 inches (1.2 meters) long and are vividly colored. They have a large bright greenish–yellow stripe, bordered in black, running the length of their body. To either side of the stripe there are red or reddish–orange stripes. The top of their heads are red, and their bellies are greenish–blue.

San Francisco garter snakes are diurnal (active during the day). They like to be warm, and during cool weather can often be found seeking out the sun. Each adult snake has its own hibernating burrow—a hole dug out by another animal or a natural crevice. Some San Francisco garter snakes estivate

One of the threats facing the San Francisco garter snake is the grave population decline of the snakes' main food source, the California red–legged frog.

(enter a dormant, or sleep–like, state) in their burrows at times in the summer when ponds have gone dry. In cooler parts of their range, particularly near the coast, the snakes hibernate in winter. Even during its periods of hibernation, if the weather is nice, the snake will come out of its burrow to lie in the sun. Where it is warmer, the snakes remain active through the seasons.

The main food of the San Francisco garter snake is the California red–legged frog (see entry in Volume 2). They also eat other frogs and toads, as well as other prey, such as earthworms and insects, which they find by foraging in the grass and leaves on the forest floors, and small fish they find in the water. These snakes are shy. When they are disturbed they tend to hide in water or under cover in the woods.

San Francisco garter snakes mate from about late March to early June. Females of this species can store the male's sperm throughout the winter. They will give birth to anywhere from 7 to 85 live infants from late June to early October.

Habitat and current distribution

San Francisco garter snakes live in moist habitats like grasslands or meadows, marshy and damp woodlands, and farms or parks that are near ponds and marshes. They are most often found around ponds that have large frog populations. They live within small areas in San Mateo County, California. Currently, there is little information about where the snakes occur, largely because they are scattered through privately owned land, although they have also been observed on county lands. Their population numbers are not known.

History and conservation measures

The San Francisco garter snake's range has always been in San Mateo County. However, it was once found in a wide sweep up and down the county and now is found only in isolated places.

The San Francisco garter snake is threatened because of habitat destruction from farming and urban development. For years it has been captured for sale to reptile collectors and traders. One of the threats facing the species is the grave population decline of the snake's main food source, the California red–legged frog. At the end of the nineteenth century, bullfrogs were introduced into the areas shared by the California red–legged frog and the San Francisco garter snake. Bullfrogs prey on California red–legged frogs and have reduced the once–abundant population to the brink of extinction, thus depriving the snakes of a vital food supply. Bullfrogs also prey upon young San Francisco garter snakes.

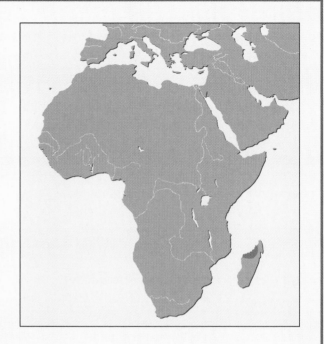

TORTOISE, ANGULATED
Geochelone yniphora

PHYLUM: Chordata
CLASS: Reptilia
ORDER: Testudines
FAMILY: Testudinidae
STATUS: Endangered, IUCN
Endangered, ESA
RANGE: Madagascar

Tortoise, angulated
Geochelone yniphora

Description and biology

The angulated tortoise, also known as the Madagascar tortoise or angonoka, is a large animal. Its rotund carapace (pronounced KAR–a–pace), or top shell, measures 18 inches (46 centimeters) long. Dark wedge–shaped markings appear across this light brown carapace. The tortoise's characteristic feature is a hornlike protuberance, or projection, that juts out underneath its neck from its plastron, or ventral (bottom) shell. A herbivore (plant–eater), the tortoise feeds mainly on leaves, grasses, and shoots.

Biologists (people who study living organisms) have very little information on the angulated tortoise's breeding habits in the wild. Those tortoises in captivity have been observed mating between October and February. Males engage in duels, apparently over the right to mate with females.

An angulated tortoise and its baby. Biologists have been able to discover little about the tortoises' breeding habits in the wild.

Habitat and current distribution

Unique to Madagascar (an island off the southeast coast of Africa), the angulated tortoise is found in a limited area around Baly Bay, in the northwestern part of the island. The tortoise prefers to inhabit a mixture of tropical deciduous (shedding trees and plants) forests and grasslands.

Since only a few hundred angulated tortoises remain in the wild, the animal is seriously threatened with extinction.

History and conservation measures

Between the seventeenth and twentieth centuries, angulated tortoises were hunted in great numbers for food. Malagasy law now protects the tortoise from such hunting, but serious threats remain. Predators, such as wild pigs, destroy the tortoises' nests. Much of the tortoises' habitat has been cleared and converted into farmland.

In 1986, the Jersey Wildlife Preservation Trust and the Department of Waters and Forests of Madagascar mounted a species recovery plan for the tortoise. The plan includes breeding the tortoise in captivity, preserving its natural habitat, and educating local people about the threat facing the tortoise.

In May 1996, 73 young tortoises and 2 adult females were stolen from the captive–breeding compound in northwestern Madagascar. Officials believed the angulated tortoises were taken to be sold illegally to collectors.

TORTOISE, DESERT
Gopherus agassizii

PHYLUM: Chordata
CLASS: Reptilia
ORDER: Testudines
FAMILY: Testudinidae
STATUS: Vulnerable, IUCN
Threatened, ESA
RANGE: Mexico, USA (Arizona,
California, Nevada, Utah)

Tortoise, desert
Gopherus agassizii

Description and biology

The desert tortoise has an oblong, domed, brown carapace (pronounced KAR–a–pace), or top shell, that measures between 7.5 and 15 inches (19 and 38 centimeters) long. Its head is narrow and scaly, and its tail is short. The tortoise has armored front legs, which it uses for digging, and large, powerful rear legs. Males of the species are much larger than females.

The desert tortoise's diet consists primarily of plants that contain a high level of water. In its desert habitat, the tortoise drinks from depressions that it often scrapes out itself to catch rainwater. The desert tortoise is active mainly in the spring. In summer, it is active when rains provide moisture and food.

During courtship, males often hiss and butt females. After mating, a female desert tortoise lays two to seven hard–shelled eggs in early summer. She covers the eggs with only a thin layer of sand, allowing the sun's heat to incubate (develop)

A desert tortoise in the Mohave Desert. The tortoise uses its front legs for digging holes in which to catch rain water for drinking.

them. The eggs hatch after three to four months. The young tortoises have soft shells that begin to harden after about five years.

Desert tortoises do not reach sexual maturity until they are 15 to 20 years of age, but can live as long as 100 years.

Habitat and current distribution

The desert tortoise is found in the Mojave and Sonoran Deserts in the southwestern United States and Mexico. Although this range is wide, the tortoise population is scattered and isolated throughout it. Biologists (people who study living organisms) believe the total desert tortoise population to be only around 100,000.

To the north and west of the Grand Canyon, desert tortoises inhabit valleys and tracts where creosote bushes (evergreen resinous desert shrub) and yucca plants grow. To the south and east of the Grand Canyon, isolated populations of tortoises inhabit steep, rocky slopes of mountain ranges where paloverde trees (small bushy trees with sharp spines) and cacti grow. Biologists are unsure of the tortoise's habitat in Mexico.

History and conservation measures

The desert tortoise was once found at lower elevations throughout the Mojave and Sonoran Deserts. Recently, however, its numbers have declined in most areas. Many factors have led to this decline. These tortoises have been illegally hunted for food or for sale as pets. Their habitat has been lost or destroyed as farms and cities have been built, roads have been constructed, mining explorations have been undertaken, and toxic and radioactive waste dumps have been established. Livestock from nearby ranches and farms have trampled their food sources, and off–road vehicles have further destroyed what remains of the animal's fragile habitat.

The desert tortoise is California's official state reptile. At present, there are two reserves in California providing protected habitats for the tortoise: the Desert Tortoise Research Natural Area and the Chuckwalla Bench Area of Critical Environmental Concern. A small reserve in Utah provides a protected habitat for a few desert tortoises.

A federal plan to save the desert tortoise was developed in 1995. However, due to a lack of money and arguments between conservationists (people protecting the natural world) and people who use the desert for recreational purposes, this plan has yet to be set in motion.

TORTOISE, GALÁPAGOS GIANT
Geochelone nigra (elephantopus)

PHYLUM: Chordata
CLASS: Reptilia
ORDER: Testudines
FAMILY: Testudinidae
STATUS: Vulnerable, IUCN
Endangered, ESA
RANGE: Ecuador
(Galápagos Islands)

Tortoise, Galápagos giant
Geochelone nigra (elephantopus)

Description and biology

The Galápagos giant tortoise is a gigantic tortoise that can weigh up to 580 pounds (263 kilograms). In certain subspecies, its top shell, or carapace (pronounced KAR–a–pace), is high and shaped like a dome. In others, the carapace is high only in front. This low–lying shell—called saddleback—flares out at the bottom. The length of a Galápagos giant tortoise varies depending on the shape of its carapace and its gender. An average saddleback female measures 24 inches (61 centimeters) long, while an average domed–shelled male measures about 50 inches (127 centimeters) long.

Galápagos giant tortoises reach sexual maturity between 20 and 30 years of age. Breeding usually takes places between January and June, the rainy season. After mating, a female Galápagos giant tortoise migrates to an arid (dry), lowland

area to lay her eggs. Beginning in June, she lays between 2 and 20 tennis–ball–shaped eggs in a nest she has dug out in the ground. She then covers the nest and returns to the highlands. The eggs incubate (develop) for four to eight months before hatching. The nest's temperature determines the offspring's sex: warmer temperatures produce more females; cooler temperatures produce more males. Between November and April, the eggs hatch and the young tortoises begin to dig their way out of the nest. At birth, they weigh about 9 ounces (255 grams), or 0.1 percent of their adult weight.

The Galápagos giant tortoise, which may live to be 100 years old, is an herbivore (plant–eater). It feeds on more than 50 different types of plants. The tortoise has a keen sense of smell, and it will smell all of its food before eating. It can survive for a long period without food or water because it can metabolize, or break down, fat stored in its tissues.

Although conservation efforts have been implemented to save the Galápagos giant tortoise, the outlook for the tortoise still remains guarded.

Habitat and current distribution

The Galápagos giant tortoise is found only on the Galápagos Islands, a province of Ecuador lying about 600 miles (965 kilometers) off the country's west coast. It inhabits the islands of Hood, Isabela, Pinzon, San Cristobal, Santa Cruz, and Santiago. Biologists (people who study living organisms) estimate that about 15,000 Galápagos giant tortoises currently exist.

This tortoise is found in various areas on these islands, from sea level to the highest points. During the dry season, the tortoise migrates to higher altitudes to find food and water. Most larger Galápagos giant tortoises are found in the higher altitudes.

History and conservation measures

Humans have been a major threat to the Galápagos giant tortoise. When Spanish navigator Tomás de Bertanga and his fellow explorers discovered the Galápagos Islands in 1535, they found so many giant tortoises there that they named the islands *Galápagos,* Spanish for "tortoise." Biologists estimate that 250,000 tortoises inhabited the islands when Bertanga and his men arrived.

In the nineteenth century, whalers and explorers who visited the islands slaughtered thousands of Galápagos giant tortoises for their meat, oil, and fat. To have fresh meat during their voyages, these men sometimes took live tortoises onboard their ships and stored them in the holds for up to a year before killing them.

The Galápagos giant tortoise is currently threatened by animals introduced by humans into the tortoise's habitat. Dogs and pigs prey on tortoise eggs and young tortoises. Goats compete with the tortoises for food. Donkeys trample or roll in tortoise nesting areas, often damaging eggs.

In 1959, the Ecuadoran government declared all uninhabited areas of the Galápagos Islands to be a national park. This act prevents any island species from being hunted, captured, or disturbed. The Charles Darwin Research Station on Santa Cruz Island has launched a program to control the predator population. Although this program has been successful, the outlook for the survival of the Galápagos giant tortoise remains guarded.

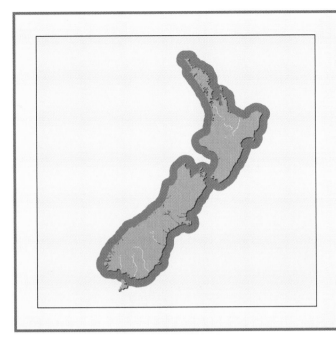

TUATARA
Sphenodon punctatus

PHYLUM: Chordata
CLASS: Reptilia
ORDER: Rhyncocephalia
FAMILY: Sphenodontidae
STATUS: Endangered, ESA
RANGE: New Zealand

Tuatara

Sphenodon punctatus

Description and biology

The tuatara (pronounced too–a–TAR–a) is a lizardlike reptile. It is olive green and speckled with yellow. It has a
medium–sized head and a strong tail. The tuatara's feet and
hands each have five clawed digits (toelike projections). A crest
of soft spines stretches along its back to the base of its tail.
An average female tuatara measures 20 inches (51 centimeters) long and weighs about 1 pound (0.45 kilogram). An average male measures 24 inches (61 centimeters) in length and
weighs about 2.6 pounds (1.2 kilograms).

The tuatara has certain physical characteristics that separate it from lizards. Among other things, it has extra holes in
its skull and bony projections on its ribs. Males of the species
lack a copulating (breeding) organ. It has a single row of teeth
in its lower jaw and a double row in its upper jaw. When the
tuatara's mouth is closed, its bottom row of teeth fit neatly
between its upper two rows. None of these teeth are replaced

when worn out or damaged. This reptile also has a third eye—called a pineal eye—on the top of its head. The eye contains a simplistic lens and retina and is connected to the brain by a nerve. Since this eye is covered by opaque scales, not much light gets through. Some biologists (people who study living organisms) believe the eye may function as a light sensor, determining how much time the tuatara spends basking in sunlight.

The tuatara is mainly nocturnal (active at night). It feeds on worms, snails, beetles, crickets, birds' eggs, small lizards, and frogs. During the day, when not basking in the sun, the tuatara spends time in burrows built as nests by shearwaters and petrels (both sea birds).

Since males do not have copulating organs, tuataras breed like birds. When mating, a male and female bring their cloacae into contact. A cloaca (pronounced klow–AH–ka) is a cavity in the body of birds, reptiles, amphibians, and most fishes that has an opening to the outside through which sperm and body wastes such as feces pass. Once having mated, a female tuatara lays a clutch of 6 to 10 eggs in a burrow or tunnel sometime between October and December. The female abandons the eggs after covering them with soil and the eggs hatch 13 to 15 months later. Tuataras can live up to 100 years.

Habitat and current distribution

The tuatara is found on about 30 islands around New Zealand. Biologists estimate that the current tuatara population is between 60,000 and 100,000. More than half of all tuataras exist on Stephens Island.

On its island habitat, the tuataras is found in forest or dense scrub areas from sea level to an altitude 1,000 feet (305 meters) above sea level.

History and conservation measures

Tuataras are the most ancient of all living reptiles. They are the last surviving members of a family of reptiles that stretches back to the early Mesozoic Era, about 200,000,000 years ago. During the age of reptiles, tuataras lived alongside dinosaurs. With the extinction of the dinosaurs 65,000,000 years ago, the age of mammals began and the tuatara soon disappeared from everywhere on Earth except New Zealand.

Humans first came to the New Zealand islands from nearby Polynesian islands sometime between 1,000 and 2,000 years ago. They brought with them the kiore, or Polynesian rat. The kiore quickly became a predator of tuatara eggs and young. As more humans came to the New Zealand islands, bringing with them predators such as pigs and cats, the tuatara suffered. By the end of the nineteenth century, the reptile had become extinct on the main islands of New Zealand.

Efforts are currently underway to remove rats from tuatara island habitats. On the island of Tiritiri Matangi, all rats have now been eliminated. The island now teems with rich plant life, insects, lizards, forest birds, and tuataras. All islands on which tuataras are found are designated either wildlife sanctuaries or flora and fauna reserves. Both of these designations limit the number of humans who can visit these islands.

TURTLE, CENTRAL AMERICAN RIVER
Dermatemys mawii

PHYLUM: Chordata
CLASS: Reptilia
ORDER: Testudines
FAMILY: Dermatemydidae
STATUS: Endangered, IUCN
Endangered, ESA
RANGE: Belize, Guatemala,
Honduras, Mexico

Turtle, Central American river

Dermatemys mawii

Description and biology

The Central American river turtle is the largest freshwater turtle in its range. An average adult measures 24 inches (61 centimeters) long and weighs almost 50 pounds (23 kilograms). The turtle has webbed feet, forcing it to move awkwardly on land. Because of this, the Central American river turtle does not bask in the sunlight on logs or river banks like other freshwater turtles. It occasionally floats on the water's surface and is able to remain underwater for long periods without surfacing for air.

This species of turtle is primarily nocturnal (active at night), remaining inactive during the day until twilight. It

feeds on aquatic plants and fallen leaves and fruit. Otters are its main predators.

In April and December, after having mated, a female Central American river turtle digs a hole in sand, clay, or mud within a few feet of the water's edge. She then lays a clutch (eggs produced at one time) of 6 to 16 hard–shelled eggs.

Habitat and current distribution

The Central American river turtle is found only in the coastal lowlands of the western Caribbean. Its range extends from the Mexican state of Veracruz southeast through Guatemala and Belize. The turtle is not found on Mexico's Yucatán Peninsula. Biologists (people who study living organisms) are unable to estimate the total number of Central American river turtles currently in existence.

Although restrictions on hunting the Central American river turtle are currently in place, they are poorly enforced. As a result, the Central American river turtle population remains in jeopardy.

Central American river turtles inhabit large, open rivers and permanent lakes. Although they prefer clear freshwater, the turtles are sometimes found in brackish water (mixture of salt water and freshwater).

History and conservation measures

The main threat to the Central American river turtle is hunting by humans. The turtle is very easy to catch and both its meat and eggs are valued by people in its range. Although large populations of the turtle remain in Belize, it is hunted in great numbers. In the southern Mexican state of Chiapas, newly built roads have opened up formerly remote areas, giving hunters greater access to turtle populations.

Restrictions on the hunting of the turtles exist, but they are poorly enforced. Programs to raise and manage the Central American river turtle as a food source are currently being studied.

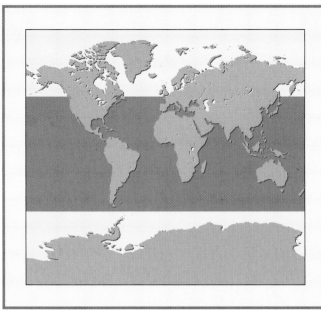

TURTLE, GREEN SEA
Chelonia mydas

PHYLUM: Chordata
CLASS: Reptilia
ORDER: Testudines
FAMILY: Cheloniidae
STATUS: Endangered, IUCN
Endangered and Threatened, ESA
RANGE: Oceanic

Turtle, green sea
Chelonia mydas

Description and biology

The green sea turtle is the largest of the hard–shelled sea turtles. An average adult weighs 300 to 350 pounds (136 to 159 kilograms) and has an upper shell, or carapace (pronounced KAR–a–pace), length of about 40 inches (102 centimeters). The large, heart–shaped carapace varies in color from dark greenish–brown to olive brown. The turtle's head is small and its front legs are large and flipper–shaped. It feeds mainly on sea grasses and algae.

Green sea turtles build nests on beaches at various times during the year depending on their location. Mating usually occurs in the water within 0.5 mile (0.8 kilometer) of the nesting beach. After mating, the female crawls slowly up on the beach at night, being very sensitive to light, sound, and other disturbances. Using her rear flippers to dig a hole, she lays her eggs, buries them with sand, then returns to the ocean. The average clutch (eggs produced at one time) size is 110 eggs,

and a female may lay between 3 and 7 clutches a season. The eggs incubate (develop) for a period of 52 to 61 days. Upon hatching, the young turtles race for the water, but are often preyed on by birds. In the water, they are preyed on by fish.

Habitat and current distribution

The green sea turtle ranges widely, having been observed as far south as Polla Island, Chile, and as far north as the English Channel. However, it is mainly a pantropical species, meaning it nests in tropical and subtropical regions. Biologists (people who study living organisms) believe there are about 150 nesting sites worldwide. Only about 10 to 15 of these sites support large populations (2,000 or more nesting females per year). The largest sites are found on Ascension Island in the southern Atlantic, western Australia, Costa Rica, Europa and

Tromelin Islands in the Mozambique Channel (strait between Madagascar and Mozambique), the Pacific coast of Mexico, the northeast coast of Oman, Pakistan, and Florida.

Because males do not leave the water, biologists have found it difficult to obtain accurate population totals for the green sea turtle. Some sources list the turtles' world population at 500,000. The breeding populations along the Pacific coast of Mexico and in Florida are the ones considered endangered. Biologists estimate that only about 300 to 400 adult females nest in Florida.

History and conservation measures

Green sea turtles have been declining in number for hundreds of years. They have always been hunted for food. In modern times, this hunting has risen with advancements in fishing technology and increases in human populations in tropical areas. Turtle eggs are collected for food; young turtles are hunted and then stuffed for souvenirs; and adults are hunted for their meat (for food), for their skins (for leather goods), and for their oil (for cosmetics).

Like other sea turtles, the green sea turtle faces the threat of nesting habitat loss. Beachfront development has decreased suitable nesting habitat for the turtle throughout its range. Even development near nesting beaches has hurt the turtle: increased shoreside lighting interferes with a female's ability to lay eggs.

Green sea turtles are often caught in shrimp nets and drown. A device called a turtle excluder device, or TED, is often used to prevent these unwanted trappings. The TED, an open–ended grid of bars, is fitted in the neck of a shrimp net. It allows small sea animals like shrimp to pass through into the bag end of the net, but prevents larger sea animals like turtles from entering. The larger animals are ejected back into open water. Although TEDs are successful in saving large sea animals, fishermen do not like to use them because they believe the TEDs limit the amount of shrimp they catch.

Because green sea turtles range across such a wide area, international cooperation is needed to conserve the species and its habitat. Agreements on how best to do that have not yet been reached.

TURTLE, LEATHERBACK SEA
Dermochelys coriacea

PHYLUM: Chordata
CLASS: Reptilia
ORDER: Testudines
FAMILY: Dermochelyidae
STATUS: Critically endangered, IUCN
Endangered, ESA
RANGE: Oceanic

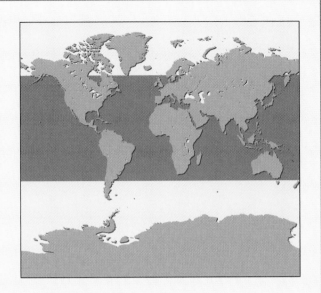

Turtle, leatherback sea
Dermochelys coriacea

Description and biology

The leatherback is the largest sea turtle in the world. An average adult can measure up to 5 feet (1.5 meters) long and weigh between 800 and 1,000 pounds (363 and 454 kilograms). Other marine turtles have hard, bony–plated shells, or carapaces (pronounced KAR–a–paces). The dark brown to black carapace of the leatherback sea turtle is made of seven raised ridges that are soft and rubbery. Its front flippers are exceptionally long and powerful. When extended, they may span over 8 feet (2.4 meters). The turtle's head and neck are dark brown or black with white or yellowish blotches.

Powerful swimmers, leatherbacks spend most of their lives at sea. They have special physical adaptations—including a thick layer of insulating fat—that allows them to stay underwater for long periods of time. Having relatively weak jaws, the turtles feed almost entirely on jellyfish, often consuming twice their weight each day.

Female leatherback sea turtles lay their eggs at different times of the year, depending on their location. Those who build nests at North Atlantic sites lay their eggs between April and July. Those at eastern Pacific sites lay theirs between November and January. After mating with a male offshore, a female leatherback crawls up on a sandy, undisturbed beach at night and digs a shallow body–pit with all four limbs. She then digs out a nest cavity about 40 inches (102 centimeters) deep with her hind limbs. She lays a clutch (eggs produced at one time) of about 100 round, white–shelled eggs in the nest, covers them with sand, then returns to the ocean.

After 56 to 65 days, the eggs hatch and the young leatherbacks, measuring 2 to 2.5 inches (5 to 6.4 centimeters) long, emerge from the nest and crawl toward the ocean. Very few survive to adulthood. Pigs, lizards, and other predators

A leatherback sea turtle sweeps up the sand with its pectoral fins before hollowing its nests.

(including humans) prey on the eggs. Before they even reach the ocean, young leatherbacks are preyed upon by birds and small mammals. In the water, both young and adult leatherbacks are preyed upon by sharks.

Habitat and current distribution

Leatherback sea turtles are among the most wide–ranging of sea animals, inhabiting waters from the tropics to the sub-arctic. They migrate vast distances to and from nesting sites. Female leatherbacks prefer to nest on relatively undisturbed beaches that have a heavy surf and deep water immediately offshore. These sites are usually located on tropical beaches in the Atlantic, Indian, and Pacific Oceans. Sometimes the turtles gather in temperate (mild) waters where jellyfish are more abundant.

Since males do not come ashore, it is almost impossible for biologists (people who study living organisms) to estimate how many currently exist. But since females do, biologists are able to count them. In the 1980s and 1990s, it was estimated that about 100,000 nesting females existed around the world. A 2000 survey showed more than 80 percent decline in nesting in the Pacific populations of the species. Estimates suggest that there has been a 70 percent reduction in the global population of adult females in less than one generation.

History and conservation measures

During the 1960s, biologists believed the leatherback sea turtle was on the verge of extinction. The turtle's population has since increased and declined. It faces many threats, including the loss of its coastal nesting habitats, entrapment in fishing nets, poaching of its eggs, and poisoning from plastics.

Many areas that were once leatherback nesting sites have been converted into living areas for humans or developed into tourist areas. Other nesting sites have been destroyed as off–road vehicles and the development of nearby land have caused beach erosion.

Turtles and other large sea animals are often caught in shrimp-fishing nets and drown. It is estimated that 11,000 sea turtles, many of them leatherbacks, are trapped this way each year. To prevent this from happening, many nets have turtle excluder devices or TEDs built into them. A TED is a grid of bars with an opening at either the top or the bottom.

This grid is fitted into the neck of a shrimp net. Small sea animals like shrimp pass easily through the bars into the bag end of the net. Large sea animals like turtles strike the bars and are ejected back out through the opening. TEDs safely remove about 97 percent of the turtles that become trapped in the shrimp nets. However, shrimpers complain that TEDs reduce the amount of shrimp they are able to catch. In the early 2000s, the U.S. government closed a large area in the Pacific Ocean to U.S. longline fishery (fishing with a line up to several miles long with a series of baited hooks along its length) in order to protect leatherbacks from being captured accidentally.

Although leatherback sea turtle meat is oily and not very appetizing, some people along the turtle's range do hunt the animal. Its eggs are especially prized in Malaysia. International trade of all sea turtle products is forbidden under the Convention on International Trades in Endangered Species (CITES), but some nations allow the use of leatherback sea turtle meat, oil, and eggs.

Plastic trash in the ocean, such as clear sandwich bags, is a grave concern because leatherbacks cannot distinguish between jellyfish and clear plastic. Recent examinations found that many turtles had plastic in their stomachs. Biologists do not know how much plastic it takes to kill a leatherback sea turtle, but no amount is beneficial, and the oceans are becoming more polluted with plastics every day.

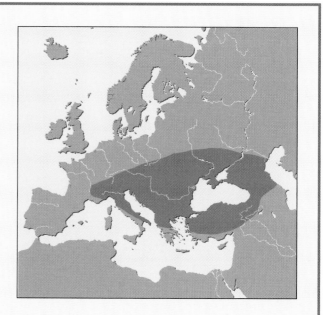

Viper, meadow
Vipera ursinii

Description and biology

The meadow viper, also called Orsini's viper, is Europe's smallest viper. It is a venomous (poisonous) snake. Males average about 16 inches (41 centimeters) long, while females are larger, up to 2 feet (60 centimeters) in length. The meadow viper preys upon insects, especially grasshoppers, as well as small mammals and lizards. Females give birth to live young (rather than laying eggs).

There are several subspecies of the meadow viper. *Vipera ursinii rakosiensis,* the subgroup found in Hungary and parts of Austria, is the most threatened, and many believe it is on the verge of extinction.

Habitat and current distribution

Meadow vipers currently exist throughout Europe, but in fragmented populations that are isolated from each other. The

species prefers either lowland meadows or southern–facing mountain pastures at elevations between 4,600 and 8,000 feet (1,400 and 2,440 meters). Meadow vipers are most often found in steppes (vast, treeless, flat tracts of land in south-eastern Europe and Asia) or semi–steppes environments. Each of the different subspecies of meadow viper has its own range, and in some areas meadow vipers remain relatively abundant, though still threatened. The highly endangered Hungarian meadow viper, *Vipera ursinii rakosiensis*, now occurs only in the Great Hungarian Plain between the Danube and Tisza rivers and in the Hansa'g Nature Reserve in the northwestern part of Hungary.

History and conservation measures

Throughout Europe, the meadow viper has been endangered by the loss and fragmentation of its habitat due to

Throughout Europe, the meadow viper has been endangered by the loss and fragmentation of its habitat due to agriculture, road–building, and livestock practices. These small snakes have also been illegally captured for trade as terrarium animals.

agriculture, road–building, and livestock practices. These small snakes have also been illegally captured for trade as terrarium (small, transparent cages, often made of glass or plastic) animals. The Hungarian subspecies of meadow viper once ranged throughout suitable habitats in Hungary, the easternmost part of Austria, Transylvania (Romania), and northern Bulgaria. The range of this subspecies has been greatly fragmented by human–related habitat disturbance. Croatia has had protective measures for the meadow viper in place since 1965.

Because the Hungarian subspecies is close to extinction, the Council of Europe Convention on the Conservation of European Wildlife and Natural Habitats Standing Committee has recommended the government of Hungary: 1) establish protected meadow habitats in the range of the existing meadow viper populations; 2) open up surrounding habitats where the species once occurred; and 3) prohibit the burning of farm land in Hungary.

Scientists believe that the Hungarian subspecies of meadow viper, because of its very low population and the isolation of the various remaining groups, is experiencing what is called *inbreeding depression*. This occurs in a small, closed population in which all individuals eventually become related to one another by descent. Over time, this will cause a loss of genetic diversity, or lower the number of biological units that pass on hereditary traits to the next generation. The effects of inbreeding depression in the wild build up over time, most seriously affecting the reproductive health of the animals, thus making them more vulnerable to extinction. One way to increase the genetic diversity among the Hungarian meadow vipers is to begin a captive–breeding program using genetically screened vipers.

Where to Learn More

Books

Ackerman, Diane. *The Rarest of the Rare: Vanishing Animals, Timeless Worlds*. New York: Random House, 1995. Naturalist and poet Ackerman travels from the Amazon rain forests to a remote Japanese island in search of endangered creatures and their habitats, revealing the factors that are contributing to their endangerment and describing preservation efforts.

Baskin, Yvonne. *The Work of Nature: How the Diversity of Life Sustains Us*. Washington, DC: Island Press, 1997. Science writer Baskin examines the practical consequences of declining biodiversity on ecosystem health and functioning, highlighting examples from around the world.

Chadwick, Douglas W., and Joel Sartore. *The Company We Keep: America's Endangered Species*. Washington, DC: National Geographic Society, 1996. Wildlife biologist Chadwick chronicles past and current conservation efforts, profiling dozens of birds and animals on the top ten endangered list. The book, for readers aged ten and above, also includes rich photographs by photojournalist Sartore, range maps, habitat descriptions, population counts, and current status for all endangered North American species.

Cohen, Daniel. *The Modern Ark: Saving Endangered Species*. New York: Putnam, 1995. Aimed at young adult readers, this work explains the problems faced by endangered species and the solutions—such as the Species Survival Plan—to help protect their futures.

Dobson, David. *Can We Save Them? Endangered Species of North America*. Watertown, MA: Charlesbridge, 1997. For students aged seven to ten, Dobson's work introduces readers to twelve species of endangered animals and plants in North America and suggests ways to restore each one's natural environment.

Earle, Sylvia. *Sea Change: A Message of the Oceans*. New York: Putnam, 1995. Marine biologist and leading deep-sea explorer Earle writes about her three decades of undersea exploration and makes an urgent plea for the preservation of the world's fragile and rapidly deteriorating ocean ecosystems.

Endangered Wildlife of the World. New York: Marshall Cavendish, 1993. Developed for young adults, this 11-volume reference set presents 1,400 alphabetical entries focusing on the plight of endangered species, with a special emphasis placed on the species of North America.

Galan, Mark. *There's Still Time: The Success of the Endangered Species Act.* Washington, DC: National Geographic Society, 1997. For young readers, this photo-essay work features plants and animals that have been brought back from the brink of extinction, primarily because of the Endangered Species Act.

Harris, Michael. *Lament for an Ocean: The Collapse of the Atlantic Cod Fishery: A True Crime Story.* Toronto, Ontario: McClelland and Stewart, 1998. A gripping journalistic exposé about the overfishing that caused the collapse of the Atlantic Cod fishery in Canada, despite the clear warnings of marine scientists.

Hoff, Mary King, and Mary M. Rodgers. *Our Endangered Planet: Life on Land.* Minneapolis, MN: Lerner, 1992. For young adult readers, Hoff's work describes the delicate ecological balance among all living things on land, the damage done by humanity in contributing to the extinction of various species, and ways of preventing further harm.

Hoyt, John Arthur. *Animals in Peril: How "Sustainable Use" Is Wiping Out the World's Wildlife.* New York: Avery Publishing Group, 1995. Hoyt, executive officer of the U.S. Humane Society, contends that conservation agencies are destroying many animal species by cooperating with local governments in a conservation policy that actually promotes slaughter, suffering, and extinction.

Liittschwager, David, and Susan Middleton, in association with the Environmental Defense Organization. *Remains of a Rainbow: Rare Plants and Animals of Hawaii.* National Tropical Botanical Garden and Nature Conservancy of Hawaii, contributers. Washington, D.C.: National Geographic, 2001. A collection of photographs of the endangered species of Hawaii, capturing the delicate balance of Hawaii's lush and rapidly deteriorating ecosystems.

Mackay, Richard. *The Penguin Atlas of Endangered Species.* New York: Penguin, 2002. A resource suitable for young adults and older, this atlas provides vital information on ecosystems, identifying wildlife, the importance of biodiversity, the transplanting of plants and animals across continents, and more. Also included in its 128 pages are case studies illustrating the major threats to biodiversity and the measures being taken to conserve the species.

Mann, Charles, and Mark Plummer. *Noah's Choice: The Future of Endangered Species.* New York: Knopf, 1995. Mann and Plummer examine the controversy over the Endangered

Species Act and call for a new set of principles to serve as a guideline for choosing which endangered species to save.

Matthiessen, Peter. *Wildlife in America*. Rev. ed. New York: Penguin Books, 1995. Acclaimed naturalist-writer Matthiessen first published this classic work on the history of the rare, threatened, and extinct animals of North America in 1959.

McClung, Robert. *Last of the Wild: Vanished and Vanishing Giants of the Animal World*. Hamden, CT: Linnet Books, 1997. For readers aged 12 and above, McClung's work profiles threatened animals around the world and discusses why they are in danger and what is being done to save them.

McClung, Robert. *Lost Wild America: The Story of Our Extinct and Vanishing Wildlife*. Hamden, CT: Shoe String Press, 1993. McClung traces the history of wildlife conservation and environmental politics in America to 1992, and describes various extinct or endangered species.

Meacham, Cory J. *How the Tiger Lost Its Stripes: An Exploration into the Endangerment of a Species*. New York: Harcourt Brace, 1997. Journalist Meacham offers a probing analysis of the endangerment of the world's pure species of tigers and the role of zoos, scientists, and politics in stopping it.

Middleton, Susan, and David Liittschwager. *Witness: Endangered Species of North America*. San Francisco, CA: Chronicle Books, 1994. Through a series of 200 color and duotone portraits, photographers Middleton and Liittschwager capture 100 species of North American animals and plants on the brink of extinction.

Patent, Dorothy Hinshaw. *Back to the Wild*. San Diego, CA: Gulliver Books, 1997. For readers aged ten and above, Patent's work describes efforts to save endangered animals from extinction by breeding them in captivity, teaching them survival skills, and then releasing them into the wild.

Pollock, Stephen Thomas. *The Atlas of Endangered Animals*. New York: Facts on File, 1993. For younger readers, Pollock's work uses maps, pictures, symbols, and text to focus on areas of the world in which human activity is threatening to destroy already endangered animal species.

Quammen, David. *The Song of the Dodo: Island Biogeography in an Age of Extinctions*. New York: Scribner, 1996. In a work for adult readers, Quammen interweaves personal observation, scientific theory, and history to examine the mysteries of evolution and extinction as they have been illuminated by the study of islands.

Schaller, George. *The Last Panda*. Chicago, IL: University of Chicago Press, 1993. Noted biologist Schaller presents an account of the four years he spent in China's Sichuan Province working to protect both panda habitat and the few pandas that remained.

Threatened Birds of the World: The Official Source for Birds on the IUCN Red List. Alison Stattersfield and David R. Capper, eds. Barcelona, Spain: Birdlife International/Lynx Editions, 2000. A comprehensive encyclopedia of endangered, threatened, or vulnerable bird species worldwide, this 852-page reference is illustrated with charts, illustrations, and photographs. Each of the 1,186 threatened birds listed in this comprehensive source receives a half-page, illustrated entry, including a range map, photos or illustrations, a discussion of why the bird is listed as threatened, and information on identification, range and population, ecology, threats, conservation, and action plans.

Tudge, Colin. *Last Animals at the Zoo: How Mass Extinctions Can Be Stopped.* Washington, DC: Island Press, 1992. Zoologist Tudge details the grim conditions many animals must overcome in their natural habitats and the bleak prospects for recovery by those already on the brink of extinction.

Weidensaul, Samuel. *The Ghost with Trembling Wings: Science, Wishful Thinking, and the Search for Lost Species.* New York: North Point Press, 2003. In a series of suspenseful stories set all over the world, the author chronicles the reappearance of some supposedly extinct animals, such as the ivory-billed woodpecker and the coelacanth. In some cases, the reappearances have actually occurred, but in others it has been wishful thinking, and many of the searches have been fruitless. The book discusses both the science and the ethics of such wishful thinking.

Wilson, Edward Osborne. *The Future of Life.* New York: Knopf, 2002. A Pulitzer-prize winning naturalist's overview of the dire problems facing the natural world today, including fascinating stories of struggling species and an imagined conversation with Henry David Thoreau at Walden Pond. Wilson makes and impassioned plea for the future, providing global strategies to save the planet.

Periodicals

Endangered Species Bulletin
  Division of Endangered Species
  U.S. Fish and Wildlife Service, Washington, DC 20240

Endangered Species UPDATE
  School of Natural Resources and Environment
  The University of Michigan, Ann Arbor, MI 48109-1115

Sierra Magazine (bimonthly)
  Sierra Club
  85 Second Street
  San Francisco, CA 94105-3441

Web Sites

Birdlife International
  http://www.birdlife.net/

Convention on International Trade in Endangered Species
  http://www.wcmc.org.uk:80/CITES/english/index.html

EcoNet: Habitats and Species
  http://www.igc.apc.org/igc/issues/habitats

EE-Link: Endangered Species, University of Michigan
  http://www.nceet.snre.umich.edu/EndSpp/Endangered.html

Endangered! Exploring a World at Risk: The American Museum
  of Natural History
  http://www.amnh.org/nationalcenter/Endangered

Endangered Species Act (brief history), University of Oregon
  http://gladstone.uoregon.edu/~cait/

Endangered Species Home Page, U.S. Fish and Wildlife Service
  http://www.fws.gov/~r9endspp.endspp.html

Endangered Species Protection Program, U.S. Environmental
  Protection Agency
  http://www.epa.gov/espp

Endangered Species Study Web: General Resources
  http://www.studyweb.com/animals/endang/endanger.htm

Endangered Species Update, University of Michigan
  http://www.umich.edu/~esupdate/

EnviroLink: Largest online environmental information resource
  http://www.envirolink.org/

Environmental Education (EE) Link: Endangered Species
  http://eelink.net/EndSpp/specieshighlights-mainpage.html

Environmental Organization Web Directory: Wildlife and endangered species focus
  http://www.webdirectory.com/Wildlife/General_Endangered
  _Species

Green Nature
  http://greennature.com

IUCN Red List of Threatened Animals
  http://www.wcmc.org.uk/data/database/rl_anml_combo.html

IUCN Red List of Threatened Plants
  http://www.wcmc.org.uk/species/plants/plant_redlist.html

SeaWorld Education Department: Endangered Species
  http://www.seaworld.org/infobooks/Endangered/home.html

Society for the Protection of Endangered Species (group of
  endangered species-related weblinks)
  http://pubweb.ucdavis.edu/Documents/GWS/Envissues
  /EndSpes/speshome.htm

Terra's Endangered Species Tour (includes range maps)
http://www.olcommerce.com/terra/endanger.html

Organizations Focusing on Endangered and Threatened Species (selected list)

African Wildlife Foundation
  1717 Massachusetts Ave., NW
  Washington, DC 20036
  (202) 265-8393; Fax: (202) 265-2361
  Internet: http://www.awf.org
  Organization that works to craft and deliver creative solutions
  for the long-term well-being of Africa's remarkable species and
  habitats.

American Cetacean Society
  P.O. Box 1319
  San Pedro, CA 90733-0391
  (310) 548-6279; Fax: (310) 548-6950
  Internet: http://www.acsonline.org
  Nonprofit organization that works in the areas of conservation, education, and research to protect marine mammals, especially whales, dolphins, and porpoises, and the oceans in
  which they live.

Animal Welfare Institute
  P.O. Box 3650
  Washington, DC 20007
  (202) 337-2332; Fax: (202) 338-9478
  Organization active in the protection of endangered species,
  among other issues, related to animal welfare.

Center for Biological Diversity
  P.O. Box 710
  Tucson AZ 85702-0710
  (520) 623-5252; Fax: (520) 623-9797
  Internet: http://www.center@biologicaldiversity.org
  A nonprofit regional conservation organization with over
  7,500 members, dedicated to protecting biological diversity
  through science, policy, education, and environmental law.
  The Center has been a premier endangered species advocate.
  It has obtained, often by filing lawsuits in the federal courts,
  ESA protection for 280 species and the designation of over 38
  million acres of critical habitat, helping to protect U.S. coasts,
  oceans, deserts, forests, rivers and grasslands for threatened
  species.

Center for Marine Conservation, Inc.
  1725 DeSales St., NW, Suite 500
  Washington, DC 20036
  (202) 429-5609; Fax: (202) 872-0619

Nonprofit organization dedicated to protecting marine wildlife and their habitats and to conserving coastal and ocean resources.

Center for Plant Conservation, Inc.
P.O. Box 299
St. Louis, MO 63166
(314) 577-9450; Fax: (314) 577-9465
Internet: http://www.mobot.org/CPC/
National network of 25 botanical gardens and arboreta dedicated to the conservation and study of rare and endangered U.S. plants.

The Conservation Agency
6 Swinburne Street
Jamestown, RI 02835
(401) 423-2652; Fax: (401) 423-2652
Organization that conducts research and gathers data specifically aimed to preserve rare, endangered, and little-known species.

Defenders of Wildlife
1101 14th St., NW, Suite 1400
Washington, DC 20005
(202) 682-9400; Fax: (202) 682-1331
Internet: http://www.defenders.org/
Nonprofit organization that works to protect and restore native species, habitats, ecosystems, and overall biological diversity.

Earthjustice Legal Defense Fund
426 17th Street, 5th Floor
Oakland, CA 94612-2820
(510) 550-6725; Fax: (510) 550-6749
Internet: http://www.eajusca@earthjustice.org
Founded in 1971 as Sierra Club Legal Defense Fund, Earthjustice is a nonprofit law firm dedicated to protecting nature by working through the courts. Earthjustice has played a leading role in shaping the development of environmental law in the courtrooms and also in Washington, D.C. where it is influential in shaping policies and legislation. The organization also runs environmental law clinics at Stanford University and the University of Denver, educating students in public interest environmental law.

Endangered Species Coalition
666 Pennsylvania Ave., SE
Washington, DC 20003
(202) 547-9009
Coalition of more than 200 organizations that seeks to broaden and mobilize public support for protecting endangered species.

Environmental Investigation Agency (EIA)
P.O. Box 53343
Washington D.C. 20009
(202) 483-6621; Fax: (202) 986-8626
Internet: http://www.EIAgency@email.msn.com
An international campaigning organization formed in 1984, committed to investigating and exposing environmental crime by using advanced investigative techniques. EIA often works undercover to expose international crimes such as illegal trade in wildlife and illegal logging. The organization has brought about changes in international and national laws and policies.

International Union for Conservation of Nature and Natural Resources (IUCN-The World Conservation Union)
U.S. Office: 1400 16th St., NW
Washington, DC 20036
(202) 797-5454; Fax: (202) 797-5461
Internet: http://www.iucn.org
An international independent body that promotes scientifically based action for the conservation of nature and for sustainable development. The Species Survival Commission (SSC) of the IUCN publishes biennial Red List books, which describe threatened species of mammals, birds, reptiles, amphibians, fish, invertebrates, and plants.

International Wildlife Coalition
70 East Falmouth Highway
East Falmouth, MA 02536
(508) 548-8328; Fax: (508) 548-8542
Internet: http://www.webcom.com/-iwcwww
Nonprofit organization dedicated to preserving wildlife and their habitats. IWC's Whale Adoption Project preserves marine mammals.

International Wildlife Education and Conservation
1140 Westwood Blvd., Suite 205
Los Angeles, CA 90024
(310) 208-3631; Fax: (310) 208-2779
Internet: http://www.iwec.org/iwec.htm
Nonprofit organization that seeks to ensure the future of endangered animals and to promote animal welfare through public education and conservation of habitats.

Marine Environmental Research Institute
772 West End Ave.
New York, NY 10025
(212) 864-6285; Fax (212) 864-1470
Nonprofit organization dedicated to protecting the health and biodiversity of the marine environment, addressing such problems as global marine pollution, endangered species, and habitat destruction.

National Audubon Society
 700 Broadway
 New York, NY 10002
 (212) 979-3000
 Internet: http://www.audubon.org
 A national network of community-based nature centers dedicated to the conservation and restoration of natural resources
 with emphasis on wildlife, habitats, soil, water, and forests,
 particularly emphasizing advocacy on behalf of areas sustain-
 ing important bird populations.

National Wildlife Federation
 Laurel Ridge Conservation Education Center
 8925 Leesburg Pike
 Vienna, VA 22184-0001
 (703) 790-4000; Fax: (703) 442-7332
 Internet: http://www.nwf.org
 Nonprofit organization that seeks to educate, inspire, and
 assist individuals and organizations of diverse cultures to
 conserve wildlife and other natural resources.

Nature Conservancy
 1815 North Lynn St.
 Arlington, VA 22209
 (703) 841-5300; Fax: (703) 841-1283
 Internet: http://www.tnc.org
 International nonprofit organization committed to preserving
 biological diversity by protecting natural lands and the life
 they harbor.

Pacific Center for International Studies
 33 University Sq., Suite 184
 Madison, WI 53715
 (608) 256-6312; Fax: (608) 257-0417
 An international think tank specializing in the assessment
 of international treaty regimes, including the Convention on
 International Trade in Endangered Species (CITES) and the
 International Convention for the Regulation of Whaling
 (ICRW).

Save the Manatee Club
 500 North Maitland Ave.
 Maitland, FL 32751
 (407) 539-0990; Fax: (407) 539-0871
 Internet: http://www.objectlinks.com/manatee
 National nonprofit organization that seeks to preserve the endangered West Indian manatee through public education, research funding, rescue, rehabilitation, and advocacy.

Wildlife Preservation Trust International, Inc.
 400 West Girard Ave.
 Philadelphia, PA 19104
 (215) 222-3636; Fax: (215) 222-2191

Organization that supports the preservation of endangered species through hands-on field work, research, education, and training.

World Conservation Monitoring Centre
219 Huntington Rd.
Cambridge, England CB3 ODL
(01223) 277314; Fax: (01223) 277136
Internet: http://www.wcmc.org.uk
Organization that supports conservation and sustainable development through the provision of information services on issues relating to nature conservation.

World Society for the Protection of Animals
29 Perkins St.
P.O. Box 190
Boston, MA 02130
(617) 522-7000; Fax: (617) 522-7077
International organization committed to the alleviation of animal suffering and to the conservation of endangered animals.

World Wildlife Fund
1250 24th St., NW
Washington, DC 20037
(202) 293-4800; Fax: (202) 293-9211
Internet: http://www.wwf.org
The largest private U.S. organization working worldwide to protect wildlife and wildlands—especially in the tropical forests of Latin America, Asia, and Africa.

Photo Credits

Photographs appearing in Endangered Species, *2nd Edition, were received from the following sources. Every effort has been made to secure permission; if omissions have been made, please contact us.*

Abbott's booby (Papasula abbotti), illustration by Patricia Ferrer. Reproduced by permission.—Addax with lowered head, photograph by Mark Boulton. Photo Researchers, Inc. Reproduced by permission.—African elephant, photograph by Mark Boulton. Photo Researchers, Inc. Reproduced by permission.—African wild dogs, photograph by Nigel J. Dennis. Photo Researchers, Inc. Reproduced by permission.—Agave Living Rock cactus (Ariocarpus agavoides), photograph. © Rick and Nora Bowers / Visuals Unlimited. Reproduced by permission.—American burying beetle, photograph. Photo Researchers, Inc. Reproduced by permission.—American crocodile, photograph by R. Cramm. Photo Researchers, Inc. Reproduced by permission.—Anas bernieri (duck), photograph. BIOS/Peter Arnold, Inc. Reproduced by permission.—Andean flamingo, photograph by Dr. M.P. Kahl. Photo Researchers, Inc. Reproduced by permission.—Atlantic cod, photograph by Tom McHugh. Photo Researchers, Inc. Reproduced by permission.—Audouin's Gull, photograph by Jose Luis G. Grande. Photo Researchers, Inc. Reproduced by permission.—Australian ant with caterpillar prey, photograph. Planet Earth Pictures Limited. Reproduced by permission.—Aye aye, photograph by Mike Dulaney. Cincinnati Zoo. Reproduced by permission.—Bactrian camel, photograph by Renee Lynn. Photo Researchers, Inc. Reproduced by permission.—Baiji dolphin's (Lipotes vexillifer), photograph. © Thomas Jefferson/ Seapics.com. Reproduced by permission.—Bald eagle, photograph by Tim & Pat Leeson. Photo Researchers, Inc. Reproduced by permission.—Baltic sturgeon, photograph by Tom McHugh. Photo Researchers, Inc. Reproduced by permission.—Bay checkerspot butterfly, photograph by Richard A. Arnold. Reproduced by permission.—Bengal tiger walking along beach, photograph by Jeff Lepore. Photo Researchers, Inc. Reproduced by permission.—Black caiman, photograph.

Cincinnati Zoo. Reproduced by permission.—Black rhinoceros, photograph by M. Philip Kahl, Jr. Photo Researchers, Inc. Reproduced by permission.—Black-capped vireo feeding babies, photograph by S. & S. Rucker. Vireo. Reproduced by permission.—Black-cheeked lovebirds, photograph by E. R. Degginger. Photo Researchers, Inc. Reproduced by permission. —Blue whale, photograph by Pieter Folkens. Planet Earth Pictures, Limited. Reproduced by permission.—Braun's rockcress, photograph. U.S. Fish and Wildlife Service. Reproduced by permission.—Bridled nailtail wallaby, photograph by Mitch Reardon. Photo Researchers, Inc. Reproduced by permission.— Bristle fern (Trichomanes radicons), photograph by E.D. Degginger. Bruce Coleman, Inc. Reproduced by permission. —Brown hyena, photograph by Tom McHugh. Photo Researchers, Inc. Reproduced by permission.—Buffy-eared marmoset (Callithrix aurita), photograph. Claus Meyer/Minden Pictures. Reproduced by permission.—Bull trout, photograph by Wade Fredenberg, U. S. Fish and Wildlife Service. Reproduced by permission.—California condor, photograph by Kenneth W. Fink. Photo Researchers, Inc. Reproduced by permission.—California Freshwater Shrimp, photograph. © 1994 Middleton/Littschwager. Reproduced by permission.— California red-legged frog (Rana aurora draytonii), photograph by Bruce Watkins. Animals Animals/Earth Scenes. Reproduced by permission.—Captive imperial Amazon parrot (Amasona imperialis-caribbean), photograph. © Frank W. Lane; Frank Lane Picture Agency/Corbis. Reproduced by permission.— Cape vultures, photograph by Nigel Dennis. Photo Researchers, Inc. Reproduced by permission.—Cave crayfish, photograph by Smith, Ken, Arkansas Natural Heritage Commission. Reproduced by permission.—Central American River Turtle, photograph by Tom McHugh. Photo Researchers, Inc. Reproduced by permission.—Central American tapir, photograph by Thor Janson. Photo Researchers, Inc. Reproduced by permission.—Chapman's rhododendron in bloom, photograph by David & Hayes Norris. Photo Researchers, Inc. Reproduced by permission.—Chatam Island Forget-Me-Not, in bloom, photograph by Brian Enting. Photo Researchers, Inc. Reproduced by permission.—Chatham Island black robin (Petroica traversi), illustration by Emily Damstra. Reproduced by permission.—Cheer pheasant, photograph by Tom McHugh. Photo Researchers, Inc. Reproduced by permission. —Cheetah, photograph by S.R. Maglione. Photo Researchers,

Inc. Reproduced by permission.—Chimpanzee, photograph by Nigel J. Dennis. Photo Researchers, Inc. Reproduced by permission.—Chinchilla, photograph by Stephen Dalton. Photo Researchers, Inc. Reproduced by permission.—Chinese alligator, photograph by Ken King. Planet Earth Pictures, Limited. Reproduced by permission.—Chinese Egret, photograph by M. Strange. Vireo. Reproduced by permission.—Chinese giant salamander, photograph. Cincinnati Zoo. Reproduced by permission.—Ciconia boyciana, photograph. BIOS/Peter Arnold, Inc. Reproduced by permission.—Coelacanth, photograph. Planet Earth Pictures, Limited. Reproduced by permission.— Cook Strait Tuatara, photograph by Tom McHugh. Photo Researchers, Inc. Reproduced by permission.—Crested honeycreeper, photograph by Jack Jeffrey. Photo Resource Hawaii. Reproduced by permission.—Culebra Island Giant, photograph by C. Kenneth Dodd, Jr., USGS. Reproduced by permission.—Dalmation pelican, photograph by Edmund Appel. Photo Researchers, Inc. Reproduced by permission.— Dama gazelle nursing baby, photograph by Joseph Van Wormer. Photo Researchers, Inc. Reproduced by permission.— Danube salmon, photograph by Hans Reinhard. Photo Researchers, Inc. Reproduced by permission.—Delhi sands flower-loving fly, photograph by Greg Ballmer. Reproduced by permission.—Desert pupfish, photograph by Tom McHugh. Photo Researchers, Inc. Reproduced by permission.—Desert tortoise, photograph by Tim Davis. Photo Researchers, Inc. Reproduced by permission.—Dugong, photograph. © Tom McHugh/Photo Researchers, Inc. Reproduced by permission.— Elephant, Asian, photograph by Ben Simon. Stock Market/Corbis. Reproduced with permission.—European Bison or Wisent (Bison bonasus), photograph by Peter Weimann. Animals Animals/Earth Scenes. Reproduced by permission.—European mink (Mustela lutreola), photograph. BIOS/Peter Arnold, Inc. Reproduced by permission.—Fanshell, inside and outside, photograph by S. David Jenike. Cincinnati Zoo. Reproduced by permission.—Fat Pocketbook pearly mussel, photograph by A.E. Spreitzer. Reproduced by permission.—Fiji Island iguana, photograph by Joseph L. Collins. Photo Researchers, Inc. Reproduced by permission.—Florida torreya, photograph by Gary Retherford. Photo Researchers, Inc. Reproduced by permission.—Fountain darter, photograph by Roger W. Barbour. Reproduced by permission.—Galapagos Hawk, photograph by Jeanne White. Photo Researchers, Inc. Reproduced by permission.—Galapagos land iguana, photograph by Margaret Welby. Planet Earth Pictures, Limited. Reproduced by permission.—Galapagos Tortoise, photograph by Francois Gohier. Photo Researchers, Inc. Reproduced by permission.—Gavial sliding on sand, photograph by Jeffrey W. Lang. Photo Researchers, Inc. Reproduced by permission.—Giant anteater, photograph by Robert J. Huffman. Field Mark Publications. Reproduced by permission.—Giant armadillo, photograph by Paul Crum. Photo Researchers, Inc. Reproduced by permission.—Giant catfish, photograph by Roland Seitre. © Roland Seitre/Peter Arnold, Inc. Reproduced by permission.—Giant Kangaroo Rat, photograph by Susan Middleton. © 1998 Susan Middleton. Reproduced by permission.—Giant panda, photograph by Tom & Pat Leeson. Photo Researchers, Inc. Reproduced by permission.—Golden bandicoot, photograph by Jiri Lochman. Planet Earth Pictures Limited. Reproduced by permission.—Golden Lion Tamarins, photograph. Cincinnati Zoo. Reproduced by permission.—Golden parakeet, photograph by Lynx Edicions. Vireo. Reproduced by permission.—Goldenrod, photograph by John MacGregor. Reproduced by permission.—Goliath frog with gold watch near head, photograph by Paul A. Zahl. Photo Researchers, Inc. Reproduced by permission.—Gorilla, posed, photograph by Jerry L. Ferrara. Photo Researchers, Inc. Reproduced by permission.—Gray fruit bat clinging to rock, photograph by Merlin D. Tuttle. Photo Researchers, Inc. Reproduced by permission.—Gray wolf howling, photograph by Myer Bornstein. Planet Earth Pictures Limited. Reproduced by permission.—Great Phillipine Eagle, photograph by Alain Evrard. Photo Researchers, Inc. Reproduced by permission.—Green pitcher plant, photograph. Photo Researchers, Inc. Reproduced by permission.—Green sea turtle, floating in water, photograph by Dr. Paula A. Zahl. Photo Researchers, Inc. Reproduced by permission.—Grevy zebra, photograph by Leonard Lee Rue III. Photo Researchers, Inc. Reproduced by permission.—Grizzly bear, photograph by Jeff Lepore. Photo Researchers, Inc. Reproduced by permission.—Guadalupe fur seal, photograph by C. Allan Morgan. Reproduced by permission.—Harvestman, photograph. U. S. Fish and Wildlife Service. Reproduced by permission.—Hawaiian crow, photograph by R. & N. Bowers. Vireo. Reproduced by permission.—Hawaiian goose, photograph by Roger Wilmshurst. Photo Researchers, Inc. Reproduced by permission. —Hawaiian hawk, photograph by Tom McHugh. Reproduced by permission.—Hawaiian monk seal, photograph. U. S. Fish and Wildlife Service. Reproduced by permission.—Hines emerald dragonfly, photograph. Reproduced by permission.—Honeycreeper, photograph by H. Douglas Pratt. Reproduced by permission.—Hoolock gibbon, southeast Asia, photograph by Tom McHugh. Photo Researchers, Inc. Reproduced by permission.—Houston toad, photograph by Joseph T. Collins. Photo Researchers, Inc. Reproduced by permission.—Humpback whale, photograph by Francois Gohier. Photo Researchers, Inc. Reproduced by permission.—Huon tree kangaroo, photograph. © Art Wolfe/ Photo Researchers, Inc. Reproduced by permission.—Iberian lynxes at a zoo in southern Spain, photograph. © Reuters New-Media Inc./Corbis. Reproduced by permission.—Indian python, photograph by Mandal Ranjit. Photo Researchers, Inc. Reproduced by permission.—Iowa pleistocene snails, photograph. U. S. Fish and Wildlife Service. Reproduced by permission.—Island fox (Urocyon littoralis santarosae), photograph. © Kennan Ward/Corbis. Reproduced by permission.—Ivory-billed woodpecker, photograph by Ken Lucas. Planet Earth Pictures, Limited. Reproduced by permission.—Jaguar, photograph by Renee Lynn. Photo Researchers, Inc. Reproduced by permission.—James River Spinymussel, photograph. A.E. Spreitzer. Reproduced by permission.—Kakapo, photograph. Photo Researchers, Inc. Reproduced by permission.—Kentucky cave shrimp, photograph. U. S. Fish and Wildlife Service. Reproduced by permission.—Kirtland's warbler, photograph by Bill Dyer. Photo Researchers, Inc. Reproduced by permission.—Koala, photograph by Robert J. Huffman. Field Mark Publications. Reproduced by permission.—Komodo Dragon, photograph. Cincinnati Zoo. Reproduced by permission.—Laysan finch in grassy area, photograph by Karl W. Kenyon. Photo Researchers, Inc. Reproduced by permission.—Laysan Teal duck (Anas layanensis) at the Houston Zoo, photograph by Mickey Gibson. Animals Animals/Earth Scenes. Reproduced by permission.—Lear's Macaws, photograph by Kenneth W. Fink. Photo Researchers, Inc. Reproduced by permission.—Leatherback sea turtle, photograph by C. Allan Morgan. Reproduced by permission.—Leopard, photograph by Gregory G. Dimijian. Photo Researchers, Inc. Reproduced by permission.—Leopard lizard, photograph by Rod Planck. Photo Researchers, Inc. Reproduced by permission.—Little wing pearly mussel, photograph by A. E. Spreitzer. All Rights Reserved.

Reproduced by permission.—Lord Howe Wood Rail, photograph by Vincent Serventy. Planet Earth Pictures, Limited. Reproduced by permission.—Madison Cave Isopod, photograph. © 1994 Middleton/Littschwager. Reproduced by permission.—Manatee (Trichechus manatus), photograph. © Douglas Faulkner/Corbis. Reproduced by permission.—Mandrill, photograph by Gregory G. Dimijian. Photo Researchers, Inc. Reproduced by permission.—Manus Island green snail (Papustyla pulchenrima), photograph. © L. Newman & A. Flowers. Reproduced by permission.—Marbled murrelet, photograph by R. L. Pitman. Vireo. Reproduced by permission.—Marine otter (Lutra felina), photograph. © Roland Seitre/Peter Arnold, Inc. Reproduced by permission.—Markhor, photograph. Cincinnati Zoo. Reproduced by permission.—Mauna Loa, photograph by Derral Herbst. Reproduced by permission.—Mauritius kestral, photograph by Nick Garbutt. Planet Earth Pictures, Limited. Reproduced by permission.—Meadow viper (Vipera ursinii rakosiensis), photograph. © Zoltan Takacs. Reproduced by permission.—Mexican prairie dog (Cynomys mexicanus), photograph by Patricio Robles Gil. Reproduced by permission.—Mongoose lemur, photograph by Tom McHugh. Photo Researchers, Inc. Reproduced by permission.—Monito gecko, photograph by C. Kenneth Dodd, Jr., USGS. Reproduced by permission.—Mountain pygmy possum, photograph by Tom McHugh. Photo Researchers, Inc. Reproduced by permission.—Musk deer, photograph by M. K. Ranjitsinh. Photo Researchers, Inc. Reproduced by permission.—Nashville crayfish, photograph. U. S. Fish and Wildlife Service. Reproduced by permission.—Nevin's barberry, photograph by Steve Junak. Reproduced by permission.—Northern white rhinoceros, photograph by Kenneth W. Fink. Photo Researchers, Inc. Reproduced by permission.—Northern bald ibis, photograph. Cincinnati Zoo. Reproduced by permission.—Northern spotted owl, photograph by Tom & Pat Leeson. Photo Researchers, Inc. Reproduced by permission.—Numbat, photograph. Photo Researchers, Inc. Reproduced by permission.—Numenius borealis, photograph. © J. Pierre Sylvestre/BIOS/Peter Arnold, Inc. Reproduced by permission.—Orangutan, photograph by Tim Davis. Photo Researchers, Inc. Reproduced by permission.—Orinoco crocodile, photograph by Tom McHugh. Photo Researchers, Inc. Reproduced by permission.—Ornithoptera alexandrae butterfly, photograph. © Francois Gilson/BIOS/Peter Arnold, Inc. Reproduced by permission.—Pallid sturgeon, photograph. U. S. Fish and Wildlife Service. Reproduced by permission.—Peregrine falcon with wings outstretched, photograph by Tim Davis. Photo Researchers, Inc. Reproduced by permission.—Piping plover, photograph by Bill Dyer. Photo Researchers, Inc. Reproduced by permission.—Plowshare tortoise with baby, photograph by Nick Garbutt. Planet Earth Pictures, Limited. Reproduced by permission.—Prairie white fringed orchid, photograph by Jim W. Grace. Photo Researchers, Inc. Reproduced by permission.—Pristis perotteti, photograph. BIOS/Peter Arnold, Inc. Reproduced by permission.—Przewalski's horse, San Diego Zoo, photograph by J. Gordon Miller. Reproduced by permission.—Puerto Rican boa (Epicrates inornata), photograph by John Mitchell. Photo Researchers, Inc. Reproduced by permission.—Puerto Rican boa, photograph. U. S. Fish and Wildlife Service. Reproduced by permission.—Puna grebe (Podiceps taczanowskii), photograph. Peter Arnold, Inc. Reproduced by permission.—Purple-winged dove (Claravis godefrida), photograph. © Luis C. Marigo/Peter Arnold, Inc. Reproduced by permission.—Pygmy hippopotamus, photograph. Cincinnati Zoo. Reproduced by permission.—Pygmy hog, photograph by Tom McHugh. Photo Researchers, Inc. Reproduced by permission.—Pygmy sculpin, photograph by Noel Burkhead. Reproduced by permission.—Pygmy-owl, photograph by Mike Wrigley, U.S. Fish and Wildlife Service. Reproduced by permission.—Queen conch on star coral, photograph by Charles V. Angelo. Photo Researchers, Inc. Reproduced by permission.—Red panda, photograph by Toni Angermayer. Photo Researchers, Inc. Reproduced by permission.—Red wolf, photograph by Tom & Pat Leeson. Photo Researchers, Inc. Reproduced by permission.—Red-cockaded woodpecker, photograph by David & Hayes Norris. Photo Researchers, Inc. Reproduced by permission.—Relict trillium, photograph by Jeff Lepore. Photo Researchers, Inc. Reproduced by permission.—Reslendent Quetzal, photograph by Gregory G. Dimijian. Photo Researchers, Inc. Reproduced by permission.—Ring pink mussel, photograph by A. E. Spreitzer. All Rights Reserved. Reproduced by permission.—Robbin's cinquefoil, photograph. U. S. Fish and Wildlife Service. Reproduced by permission.—Rothchild's starling, photograph. Cincinnati Zoo. Reproduced by permission.—Salt water crocodile, photograph by Tom McHugh. Photo Researchers, Inc. Reproduced by permission.—San Francisco Garter snake (Thamnophis sirtalis tetrataenis), photograph by Paul Freed. Animals Animals/Earth Scenes. Reproduced by permission.—Santa Cruz salamander, photograph. Cincinnati Zoo. Reproduced by permission.—Scimitar-horned oryx, photograph by Tom McHugh. Photo Researchers, Inc. Reproduced by permission.—Seychelles Magpie Robin, photograph by Pete Oxford. Planet Earth Pictures, Limited. Reproduced by permission.—Short-tailed albatross, photograph by Gilbert S. Grant. Photo Researchers, Inc. Reproduced by permission.—Shortnose Sucker, photograph by Joseph Tomelleri. Cimarron Trading Co. Reproduced by permission.—Siberian cranes, photograph. Planet Earth Pictures, Limited. Reproduced by permission.—Sichuan hill-partridge (Arborophila rufipectus), illustration by Bruce Worden. Reproduced by permission.—Silver rice rat (Oryzomys argentatus), photograph by Numi C. Mitchell. The Conservation Agency. Reproduced by permission.—Skinheads, photograph. Corbis. Reproduced by permission.—Small whorled pogonia flower, photograph. © Hal Horwitz/Corbis. Reproduced by permission.—Snow leopards, photograph. Cincinnati Zoo. Reproduced by permission.—Somali wild ass (Equus africanus), photograph. © Steve Kaufman/Corbis. Reproduced by permission.—Spiral aloes, photograph by Robert Story. Planet Earth Pictures Limited. Reproduced by permission.—Squirrel Monkey with baby on back, photograph. Planet Earth Pictures, Ltd. Reproduced by permission.—Steller sea lion (Eumetopias jubatus), photograph by Yva/Eastcott Momatiuk, John (Eastcott/Momatiuk). Animals Animals/Earth Scenes. Reproduced by permission.—Stirrup shell, photograph by A. E. Spreitzer. All Rights Reserved. Reproduced by permission.—Sun bear, photograph by Tom McHugh. Photo Researchers, Inc. Reproduced by permission.—Swamp deer, photograph by Tom McHugh. Photo Researchers, Inc. Reproduced by permission.—Texas blind cave salamander, photograph by Charles E. Mohr. Photo Researchers, Inc. Reproduced by permission.—Texas Wildrice, photograph by Paul M. Montgomery. All Rights Reserved. Reproduced by permission.—Tooth cave spider, photograph. U. S. Fish and Wildlife Service. Reproduced by permission.—Vancouver Island Marmot, photograph by Fletcher and Baylis. © Fletcher & Baylis/Photo Researchers, Inc. Reproduced by permission.—Venus flytrap, photograph by J.H. Robinson. Photo Researchers, Inc. Reproduced by permission.—Vicunas, mother and baby, photograph. Photo Re-

Index

Italic *type indicates volume numbers;* **boldface** *type indicates main entries and their page numbers; (ill.) indicates illustrations.*